MACMILLAN MODERN DRAMATISTS

Macmillan Modern Dramatists
Series Editors: *Bruce King* and *Adele King*

Published Titles

Eugene Benson, *J. M. Synge*

Normand Berlin, *Eugene O'Neill*

Neil Carson, *Arthur Miller*

Ruby Cohn, *New American Dramatists, 1960–1980*

Bernard F. Dukore, *Harold Pinter*

Frances Gray, *John Arden*

Julian Hilton, *Georg Büchner*

Susan Bassnett-McGuire, *Luigi Pirandello*

Leonard C. Pronko, *Eugène Labiche and Georges Feydeau*

Theodore Shank, *American Alternative Theatre*

Nick Worrall, *Nikolai Gogol and Ivan Turgenev*

Further titles in preparation

MACMILLAN MODERN DRAMATISTS

LUIGI PIRANDELLO

Susan Bassnett-McGuire

M

First published 1983 by
THE MACMILLAN PRESS LTD
London and Basingstoke
Companies and representatives throughout the world

Printed in Hong Kong

ISBN 0 333 30517 5 (hc)
ISBN 0 333 30518 3 (pbk)

Contents

List of Plates

Acknowledgements

The writing of this book may be seen as another episode in a long relationship with Pirandello. My thanks are due to Agostino Lombardo, of the University of Rome, who first encouraged me to work on Pirandello many years ago and who remains the critic whose views I most deeply care about. More recently, I should like to acknowledge the invaluable help of my colleagues in the British Pirandello Society, especially Felicity Firth, Jennifer Lorch, to whom this book is dedicated, and Jennifer Stone. My thanks also to my colleague in Theatre Studies at the University of Warwick, Clive Barker, and to Sandro d'Amico.

I am grateful to Bruce and Adele King for shrewd editing, and to Christine Wyman who typed the manuscript. Above all, as with all my work, my thanks are due to those women who have enabled me to have the physical time to write – my daughter, Lucy, my mother Eileen, Stella Dixon, and Anne Dees and Carol Miles of the University of Warwick crèche.

Author's Note

Where references to plays in the text include dates in brackets, these dates give the year of first Italian publication.

Editors' Preface

The *Macmillan Modern Dramatists* is an international series of introductions to major and significant nineteenth- and twentieth-century dramatists, movements and new forms of drama in Europe, Great Britain, America and new nations such as Nigeria and Trinidad. Besides new studies of great and influential dramatists of the past, the series includes volumes on contemporary authors, recent trends in the theatre and on many dramatists, such as writers of farce, who have created theatre 'classics' while being neglected by literary criticism. The volumes in the series devoted to individual dramatists include a biography, a survey of the plays, and detailed analysis of the most significant plays, along with discussion, where relevant, of the political, social, historical and theatrical context. The authors of the volumes, who are involved with theatre as playwrights, directors, actors, teachers and critics, are concerned with the plays as theatre and discuss such matters as performance, character interpretation and staging, along with themes and contexts.

Editors' Preface

Macmillan Modern Dramatists are written for people interested in modern theatre who prefer concise, intelligent studies of drama and dramatists, without jargon and an excess of footnotes.

BRUCE KING
ADELE KING

For Jennifer, in sisterhood

speaker is that not all Pirandello's works have been translated into English. During his long life time (1867–1936) which saw the unification of Italy, the First World War and the rise to power of Mussolini and Hitler, Pirandello produced a huge output of 6 collections of poetry, 7 novels, 14 collections of short stories, 27 full-length plays, 16 one-act plays, translations and critical essays. There has not, as yet, been a full-scale translation project to produce an English edition of the complete works, with the result that English readers have access to only a part of Pirandello's opus. One consequence of this has been that the English-language assessment of Pirandello has led to rather different conclusions than the Italian process of evaluation. English readers are almost completely unfamiliar with Pirandello's later plays, for example, and indeed Pirandello's reputation as an 'experimental dramatist' tends to be based on *Six Characters in Search of an Author* (1921). The other two plays forming the so-called 'trilogy of the theatre in the theatre', *Each in His Own Way* (*Ciascuno a suo modo*) (1924) and *Tonight We Improvise* (*Questa sera si recita a soggetto*) (1930) are not so well-known in English, although they are perhaps more radically innovative. Of plays appearing from 1927 onwards, when the great boom period of Pirandello's popularity in Europe and the United States was beginning to fade, little is known, perhaps because in several cases the English translations are so bad as to be unreadable, let alone actable. Yet it is to this period that a range of very complex and interesting plays belong: *The New Colony* (*La nuova colonia*) (1928); *Lazarus* (*Lazzaro*) (1929) – the only one of Pirandello's plays to have its première in England, at the Theatre Royal, Huddersfield on 9 July 1929; *Either Somebody's or Nobody's* (*O di uno o di nessuno*) (1929); *As You Want*

2

Me (*Come tu mi vuoi*) (1930); *Tonight We Improvise* (*Questa sera si recita a soggetto*) (1930); *Finding Oneself* (*Trovarsi*) (1932); *When One is Somebody* (*Quando si è qualcuno*) (1933); *You Don't Know How* (*Non si sa come*) (1935); *A Dream, But Perhaps it Isn't* (*Sogno, ma forse no*) (1936); *Bellavita* (1937); *The Tale of the Changeling* (*La Favola del figlio cambiato*) (1938); *The Mountain Giants* (*I giganti della montagna*) (1938).

These plays, reflecting major changes in Pirandello's style, shed a great deal of light on his career as a dramatist and deserve to be better known outside Italy. *The Mountain Giants*, Pirandello's one unfinished play, is also significant in that the production by Giorgio Strehler at the Piccolo Teatro di Milano in 1967 is a milestone in Italian theatre history, yet at present it is only available in a poor American translation by Marta Abba, the actress for whom many of Pirandello's plays were written, published in 1958.

The first problem for the English reader, then, is one of access to the works, and in spite of the great achievement of Frederick May, who almost single-handedly popularized Pirandello in the late 1950s to early 1960s in England and translated both prose and plays, often for the first time, there is still a great gap between the Italian Pirandello and the English one, where his reputation has been built upon the selected work of random translators.

Performing Pirandello's plays in English

During the process of translating from one language into another changes occur that cannot be avoided. Since no two cultures and no two languages are exactly the same, the text produced by a translator cannot by definition be the same as the original text, and translators often feel that the losses incurred in the translation process outweigh the gains that are also made. In spite of this obvious dilemma for the translator, however, some translations are easier and more fluent to read than others, some are 'actable' whilst others, although supposedly produced for the stage, are wooden and unusable. In the case of Pirandello, problems of translation seem to have loomed very large, with the result that even those plays that *can* be read in English often appear flat and downright boring.

To see a Pirandello play performed in Italian, when the range of comic devices surrounding the often pitifully tragic situations of the plot line can be fully experienced, is very different from seeing the same play performed in English. In the translation process much of the comedy seems to get lost, giving the impression to English audiences that Pirandello is a pedantic and wordy dramatist. The fact that Pirandello might be funny as well as profound does not seem to be apparent from most of the English translations, so it is small wonder that in spite of his reputation Pirandello has not been produced in English to anything like the extent that Ibsen, Strindberg or Chekhov have been.

In a useful article entitled 'Right You Are (If You Could Only Think So)', Clive Barker discusses why Pirandello has been so infrequently performed in Britain.[1] His argument is based on the anti-theoretical nature of British theatre practice; he notes that his composite image of British Pirandello, following the various productions he has seen over the past thirty years, adds up to the conclusion that:

Pirandello is tediously slow and arid, shot through with

splurges of emotional outbursts unsupported by any structural development in the action. The general impression I have is of a long time spent over little, shallow content with actors striking melodramatic poses along the way. I have come to dread the appearance of Madame Pace as no other character in the dramatic canon.

This view is no doubt shared by many who find difficulty in equating Pirandello's mighty reputation with the rare tedious performances they may see in English. Yet it would be unfair to attribute this situation only to the defects of the translators, for there have, of course, been some useful translations and some interesting performances of Pirandello over the years, and there are various other contributing factors to the difficulties.

Clive Barker has talked about the anti-intellectual bias of British theatre and the need for actors to find a 'Pirandello style' that avoids histrionics or caricature. Added to these problems is the long history of critical evaluation of Pirandello's theatre, which has tended to stress the 'cerebral' qualities of his work, and to see the plays as a series of highly intellectualized debates on the nature of Life and Art and the impossibility of communication. There is little difficulty in sustaining such a view if the texts are considered primarily as reading pieces rather than as works intended for performance and if much is made of the philosophizing of many of the characters. A different picture would emerge, however, if Pirandello's own instructions were to be followed and the so-called philosophical speeches were deliberately delivered in a different acting style to emphasize their theatricality. In other words, instead of hinging the plays on the philosophical speeches and treating the long runs of comic exchange as interludes, many of Pirandello's plays are designed as comedies broken by moments of internalized debate, whilst others, such as *Six Characters*, offer that debate through highly argumentative scenes, when the 'intellectualizing' emerges through violent verbal argument that moves at a rapid pace.

Pirandello's status as a great dramatist and the weight of critical opinion as to the intellectual content of his plays, have served as inhibiting factors for translators in the past. Again and again the simplicity of Pirandello's work, his fast-moving dialogue, carefully structured linear plots and expert use of theatrical effects are turned into something slow and ponderous when transposed into English. A glance at the titles of his plays shows something of this process at work, for it is immediately obvious that Pirandello favoured the phrase-title, the comic twist that would reveal nothing and yet simultaneously speak volumes. *Come tu mi vuoi*, the play written in 1930 for Marta Abba and based on a favourite Pirandellian theme, the relativity of identity, has as its English title *As You Desire Me*. Literally, the phrase means 'however you like/want me'; it is a colloquial phrase that invites the slightest shrug of the shoulders when spoken, and carries with it the sense both of the speaker wishing to accommodate the listener and at the same time not really caring what the response will be. But the English, by its formal register and use of the word 'desire' has moved away from the colloquial and the casual. The title has acquired a seriousness, a weight that only exists in English. The tone of the play has been altered before the reader begins to read or the audience enters the theatre.

Published in 1918, but produced two years earlier, *Cosi è, se vi pare* is one of Pirandello's best known plays, both at home and abroad. Again it deals with the problem of the relativity of identity, with the impossibility of determining exactly who someone might be. It has been translated several times into English, the first being in 1922, and is presently known by two titles: *Right You Are (If You Think So)* and *It is So (if you think so)*, the latter being the title given by the first translator, Arthur Livingston. Again the problem concerns the casual and colloquial nature of the Italian phrase, which neither English version manages to reproduce. Livingston's version is less successful because the register is so restrictedly formal, while the second title attempts to unite British colloquialism with a rather stately conditional phrase. Neither comes very near to the Italian, which could be translated roughly as 'That's it (if that's what *you* think)' or 'That's how it is (if you see it that way)', and the note of intense seriousness that characterizes English versions of Pirandello can already be heard. The joky, almost flippant tone of the Italian has undergone a sea change into something much more proper and elevated.

In spite of these difficulties, however, there have been attempts to familiarize English and American audiences with Pirandello's plays, and it is possible to isolate two distinct periods of popularity. The first coincides with his sudden rise to fame following the Italian première of *Six Characters*; Pirandello was then fifty-four years old, already moderately well-known in Italy for his prose writings and his critical dispute with Benedetto Croce, Italy's most distinguished literary critic, whose dislike of Pirandello was to endure until his death. The famous première of *Six Characters* at the Teatro Valle, Rome, on 10 May 1921, where the author was booed and scenes of violent arguing took place inside and outside the theatre, was followed by a surge of interest in the play. In 1923, George Pitoëff staged *Six Characters* at the Théâtre des

Champs-Elysées in Paris, an event that caused Lugnè-Poe to announce that a new era of the theatre had been inaugurated, and the Paris success was followed by other successful productions around the world. Writing to his daughter, Lietta, about the American *Six Characters*, Pirandello noted that the impresario had had to hire a larger theatre than anticipated because of the huge public response and furthermore 'the first volume of the plays published by Dutton is a best-seller: they sold 500 copies in a week.' In Britain the private Stage Society version of *Six Characters*, performed in 1922 when the Lord Chamberlain deemed the play too obscene for public performance, was followed in 1925 by a successful tour of four plays by Pirandello's own company in what came to be called the Pirandello Season at the New Oxford Theatre, London.

Productions of Pirandello's plays in English continued enthusiastically until 1927–28, when interest began to wane. During this period of greatest popularity, reviewers in England and America commented on Pirandello's links with Expressionism and attempted to trace connections between his plays and the work of other dramatists. Pirandello was declared to have influenced Bernard Shaw, Lennox Robinson, Sutton Vane, Noel Coward, to name but four, a list that was later to include Thornton Wilder and Tennessee Williams and many others, often on the flimsiest of pretexts.

What emerges from reviews and articles on Pirandello in English in the 1930s is either an emphasis on the subject matter of the plays or undue stress on the 'experimental form' of one play in particular, *Six Characters*, and this seems to derive from an apparent inability to perceive that a main line in Pirandello's work is the investigation of theatre form through the use of that form. So critics tried to decipher the plays, related them to Einstein's theory of relativity, just becoming popular in its own right – there was a much publicized meeting between Pirandello and Einstein at one point, but nothing they discussed has been recorded – and hailed the 'experimental' *Six Characters* as greater than *Right You Are (If You Think So)* or *To Clothe the Naked (Vestire gl'Ignudi)*. The one play reviewers and critics did seem able to come to terms with, however, was *Henry IV* (*Enrico IV*) known in America as *The Living Mask*. This play, with its tragi-comic protagonist, a perfect part for a great actor and, in fact, written for the famous Ruggero Ruggeri in 1921, was hailed as the Italian *Hamlet* and has remained the most frequently performed of all Pirandello's works in English.

In Britain, thanks to Frederick May, there was a second boom period of interest in Pirandello in the late 1950s, just at the time when the new European theatre of Beckett and Ionesco was being discovered. Reviews in England and America through the 1950s and early 60s show a shift in attitudes to Pirandello, who now came to be admired on intellectual grounds for his portrayal of man's existential plight rather than because he chose to express that plight in the theatre. By the mid-1960s Pirandello was established as a kind of precursor of the Theatre of the Absurd, with critics at pains to prove either his direct or his indirect influence on most contemporary dramatists, a vogue that continued for some considerable time. Martin Esslin and Robert Brustein both credit Pirandello with anticipating a great range of writers, from Anouilh to Genet, Sartre to Beckett and Pinter. Pirandello's place in the canon was assured.

Pirandello and Fascism

Between the two peak periods of English language interest in the theatre of Pirandello is a stretch of some twenty-five years, during which time Italy invaded Abyssinia and sent troops of Blackshirts to fight alongside Franco in the Spanish Civil War, a trail of violence and warfare that was to lead eventually to Italy's alliance with Nazi Germany. After the fall of Mussolini in 1943 and the ensuing civil strife, together with the invasion of Italy by Allied troops, the long and painful process of rebuilding began as Italians sought their way out of the residue of nearly a quarter of a century of Fascist rule. Part of that process of reconstruction was at first to reject and then, much later, as late as the 1970s in some cases, to begin a reappraisal of the work of Fascist writers and sympathisers, in which category Pirandello must be placed.

Pirandello's relationship to Fascism is problematic, but cannot be ignored. The falling-off in popularity of Pirandello's works in the 1930s and 40s is not unconnected to Anglo-American attitudes towards Fascist militarism and it does not help to try to pretend that Pirandello's overt declarations of support for Mussolini did not really happen. Eric Bentley, for example, in his edition of five plays, entitled *Naked Masks*, and still one of the most accessible small volumes of Pirandello's works in English, tries to gloss over the issue claiming that:

> it would be either a stupid or an over-ingenious critic who would stamp any of these works as fascist. They illustrate at most the plight of the playwright in a fascist state.[2]

But in an article that boldly tackles the question of

Pirandello's implicit ideological position, Jennifer Stone points to changes that occur within Pirandello's writing when Fascism had become the discourse in power.[3] She argues that Pirandello moves away from an earlier concern with the dialectics of illusion and reality towards a point of fixity where, in the last plays, elaborate patterns of symbolism come into use and dream and reality merge, no longer in conflict. The bitter laughter of the Stepdaughter at the end of *Six Characters* or of Laudisi at the end of *Right You Are* ceases to be heard in the later plays. Instead, at the end of *Lazarus* there is a miracle, at the end of *The New Colony* the heroine and her baby survive the destruction of the world alone on a mountain top, while *When One is Somebody* ends with the protagonist so locked in isolation that he physically becomes a statue of himself.

Pirandello joined the Fascist party in 1924, shortly after the murder of Giacomo Matteotti, the Socialist deputy, by Right-wing extremists. Matteotti's murder caused a great scandal and a wave of anti-Fascist feeling swept across Italy, yet it was precisely at this time that Pirandello chose to join the party and to join it with maximum publicity, giving a copy of his letter to Mussolini to the Fascist newspaper *L'Impero* (*The Empire*). Pirandello's letter was precise and to the point:

Your Excellency,

I feel that this is the most propitious moment for me to declare a loyalty which I have hitherto observed in silence. If Your Excellency finds me worthy to join the National Fascist Party I will consider it the greatest honour to become one of your humblest and most obedient followers. With utter devotion.

Response to Pirandello's public declaration of support sparked off a series of attacks and counter-attacks in the Italian press, an account of which is given in Gaspare Giudice's biography of Pirandello. What seems to be clear, however, is that at the moment of publicly declaring support for Mussolini, Pirandello was acting not out of expediency, but out of a genuine sense of conviction. His correspondence with Mussolini regarding the Arts Theatre project of 1925 shows the same spirit of enthusiasm as the *Impero* letter, and in 1935 he gave a speech at the Teatro Argentina in the presence of Mussolini, appealing for understanding from the world for Italy's invasion of Ethiopia. Such gestures and statements are not the half-hearted acquiescence of an intellectual in search of the quiet life.

Yet there are contradictions, as Giudice points out.[4] Pirandello continued to insist throughout his life that art and politics were separate, and when elected to the Academy in 1929 he gave a speech attacking d'Annunzio, the Fascist poet par excellence. He also chose, for a number of years, to travel extensively and virtually to live abroad, a fact that has been taken as a tacit expression of dissatisfaction with the regime at home. Certainly his final request for there to be no funeral and for his death not to be mentioned in the papers by friends or enemies is a long way from the celebratory pomp and ceremony that was so much a part of public Fascist manifestations.

Pirandello's Sicilian background

What should not be forgotten when considering Pirandello's acceptance of Mussolini's formula for a new and glorious Italy is that Pirandello was born in Sicily and remained deeply conscious of his Sicilian origins throughout his life. He may be justly considered as a bilingual writer, producing works in Italian and in Sicilian (debate amongst linguists still fails to agree as to whether Sicilian may be said to be a separate language or a dialectal form of Italian) and at times translating in and out of both languages. Besides writing in dialect, Pirandello also wrote theoretical articles on the state of Sicilian theatre and on dialect theatre in general, arguing for the vitality of a language in use as opposed to a language of artifice.

Whilst it would be over-simplistic to argue for a relationship between Sicilian national consciousness and the particular brand of nationalism inspired by Mussolini, the common bond between the two is the idea of forging a new sense of pride based on a restoration of almost mythical past greatness. The appeal of the myth of the great Roman Empire in a society still in the process of organizing so soon after unification in 1870 should not be under-estimated, and likewise in Pirandello's vision of Sicily the greatness of the Roman Empire combines with that of the Greeks who colonized the island. In the preface to Pirandello's Sicilian translation of Euripides' *The Cyclops*, *'U Ciclopu*, it is stated that Sicilian is the logical language for it to be translated into:

> ... Euripides' *Cyclops* could not have been more legitimately translated into any other language but Sicilian dialect. And not only because the action takes place in Sicily, but also because the Greek poet's works, in everything that goes to make up the essential *virtù* of his poetry, is still alive down there for the most part in the life of the island.

There is a great deal of critical and biographical work, most of it in Italian, on Pirandello's Sicilian background.

Sicilian characters and landscapes reappear throughout Pirandello's work, and the code of honour that forces so many of his characters to lead lives of anguish and deception reflects the restrictive provincial codes of small Sicilian towns. Olga Ragusa sums up nicely the extent to which Pirandello's Sicilian origins colour his work:

> The history, the landscapes, the social and psychological situations of Sicily appear in their undisguised, documentary reality in many of Pirandello's works. In many others they are attenuated and generalized, no more than a colouring or glow that points back through analogy to facts and circumstances actually or potentially experienced.[5]

Pirandello was born in Sicily, in a farmhouse between Agrigento and Porto Empedocle, on 28 June 1867, seven years after Garibaldi and his Redshirts had landed on the island and the Kingdom of the Two Sicilies had been joined to the northern domains of Victor Emanuel of Savoy to form the new Kingdom of Italy. As Pirandello's father was involved in one of the few lucrative industries of the island, sulphur mining, the young Pirandello grew up in a moderately comfortable bourgeois household. He began his university studies at Palermo, reading law, later moving to Rome and finally to Bonn, where he wrote a thesis on the phonetic development of the Agrigento dialect, an indication of how his tastes were shifting. His literary career had started young, with the publication of his first short story, *La capanetta* (*The Little Hut*), in a Turin newspaper at the age of seventeen, and after his Bonn degree he settled in Rome, teaching at the Magistero and writing for a living. He was never to return to live in Sicily, but the early formative years of his life stamped an indelible Sicilian-ness on his soul. In the paper setting out his last wishes he wrote:

> Burn me. And as soon as my body has been burnt the ashes must be thrown to the winds, for I want nothing, not even my ashes, to remain. But if this cannot be done the funeral urn must be taken to Sicily and walled into some rough stone near Agrigento, where I was born.

Marriage, jealousy and Pirandello

In his biography of Pirandello, Giudice discusses the impact of Sicilian social convention and its rigid formality. The Catholic ideal of virginity and the equation of honour with chastity is a motif that recurs throughout his works; a series of plays written between 1917 and 1925 hinge on the conflict between public respectability and private honour. One of his very earliest plays, *Think it over, Giacomino* (*Pensaci, Giacomino*) (1916), based on a short story, appeared in both Italian and Sicilian. The plot provides a classic example of the favoured Pirandellian theme of the clash between privately held values and public opinion.

Agostino Toti, an old schoolmaster with an overwhelming love of humanity, marries Lillina, a young girl thrown out of the house by her callous parents when they discover she is pregnant and therefore '*disonorata*' (dishonoured). Toti not only gives her his name and the comfortable house he has inherited, but he agrees to be husband in name only so that Lillina can continue to meet her lover, Giacomino Delisi, every day in the privacy of her own home. A child, Ninì, is born, adored by Toti, and the situation would seem to be ideally happy all round. Toti even finds Giacomino a job in the local bank as part of his plan to allow the lovers to live as fully as possible. But the

forces of respectability personified by Lillina's heartless
parents, the headmaster of Toti's school, whom we first
encounter in Act I complaining about Toti's lack of
discipline, Rosaria, Giacomino's fanatically religious
sister, and Padre Landolina, one of Pirandello's most
explicitly anti-clerical portraits, unite to try and put an end
to what they perceive as the scandal of the village. Act II
opens when things have begun to go wrong; we learn that
Giacomino has stopped coming to Toti's house to see
Lillina and the little boy and has not turned up for work
either. Slowly but surely, as various characters come to the
house either to gloat or to try to appeal to Toti's 'reason',
Toti understands that pressure has been brought to bear on
Giacomino to turn respectable too. The act ends with Toti
taking the little boy and going off in search of Giacomino,
as Cinquemani and Marianna, Lillina's parents, try in vain
to prevent him:

> TOTI: (*pushing him aside*) Out of the way. Let me get
> on.
> CINQUEMANI: Dear God, think what you're doing. Do
> you want to make yourself a laughing stock? I'll
> stop you.
> MARIANNA: How dare you do this? Putting on a false
> face in front of everybody?
> TOTI: (*pushing them aside, breaking free and leaving
> with the child*) Out of the way, I said. False face
> indeed. Yours are the false ones, believe me. Let me
> through.

In this exchange we see the typical Pirandellian dichotomy
between public and private honesty: Toti's honesty and
generosity are perceived as absurd and indecent by his
fellow villagers, and he in turn perceives their sense of

respectability as the most extreme form of hypocrisy. The word *maschera*, translated here as 'false face' but meaning also 'mask' or 'disguise', is likewise a word that recurs again and again through Pirandello's works. The mask, an acting device, is the falsity behind which individuals hide; it is the symbol of the insubstantiability of truth.

In the third act Toti confronts Giacomino, who is in hiding at his sister's house, and learns that he is hoping to marry a respectable young woman. Warning him to think carefully about what he is about to do, Toti convinces Giacomino that if he goes ahead with his plans he will destroy Lillina's happiness, together with that of his own son, little Ninì. Faced with this kind of moral pressure, Giacomino succumbs and Toti returns to Lillina with Giacomino and Ninì. The final moments of the play recall Orpheus leading Eurydice from the underworld. Again the savage anticlericalism that has marked the play so strongly comes to the fore. By the end of the play Toti, the old man whose unconventional living arrangements have brought happiness to all concerned, becomes the champion of the individual's right to live according to his own laws rather than to follow those laid down by social and religious convention. This reversal of values, which is both comic and heavily ironic, is a pronounced feature of Pirandello's earlier plays, and must have been very disquieting in its day.

Discussing the extent to which Pirandello's Sicilian upbringing shaped his life, Giudice makes the following statement:

for Pirandello, formality was always to be the net which excluded men from liberty. Yet he was born in a country, a world, and a century when formality was predominant. Pirandello's life and work, therefore were

17

composed of a mass of compromises and were torn between the acceptance of conventions and proprieties, and a still more fundamental rejection of them.

In the clash between Professor Toti and Landolina, the village priest, the two sides of that debate can clearly be seen, with the individualist struggling against the weight of formal tradition that dictates the patterns of life. *Think it over, Giacomino* does at least end with an apparent victory for individualism, but the dice are loaded against that victory being permanent.

The equation of chastity with honour, a deep-rooted Sicilian convention, occurs frequently in Pirandello, as does the connected theme of adultery and betrayal. In Pirandello's works characters are many times driven by sexual jealousy over real and imagined betrayals to commit acts of violence; it is tempting to relate the fondness for this kind of theme to Pirandello's own tragic marriage.

In 1894 he married Antonietta Portulano, the daughter of his father's business partner. The couple had three children, Stefano, born in 1895, Lietta, born in 1897 and Fausto, born in 1899. In 1897 he had also obtained his teaching post at the Magistero (the university faculty for training teachers) in Rome and was only a few years away from his first international success, in 1904, with the publication of his novel *The Late Mathias Pascal* (*Il fu Mattia Pascal*). But in 1903 serious flooding in the sulphur mines caused the loss of both Pirandello's father's capital and Antonietta's dowry, a shock which, according to biographers, led to the first attack of the psychic illness that was to last the rest of her lifetime. Over the years Antonietta developed an acute persecution mania, which led to pathological jealousy of her husband and daughter. Finally, in 1918, when Pirandello's son Stefano, who had been a prisoner of war, was released and returned to Rome, the family took the decision to put Antonietta into a nursing home, where she remained until her death over thirty years later.

The removal of his wife to a nursing home coincided with the beginning of Pirandello's big breakthrough into the world of the theatre. In 1918 he published *Cap and Bells* (*Il berretto a sonagli*) and *By Judgement of the Court* (*La Patente*), two one-act plays, also *The Pleasure of Honesty* (*Il piacere dell'onesta*) and a play that was to become one of his most famous, *Right You Are (If You Think So)* (*Cosi è, se vi pare*). Between 1919 and 1929 he wrote another twenty-five plays and formed his own company; in that process of writing he gradually moved on from the theme of public versus private concepts of honour to explore more widely. It is as if he ceased to focus so intensely on the problems raised by marriage as an institution, though he never abandoned his taste for the irony of that institution, which seeks to circumscribe the forces of human emotion within the bounds of social convention and property rights. After 1923, however, the emphasis of most of his plays is not so domestic.

Pirandello and practical theatre

Numerous critics have pointed out the shift in Pirandello's writing after he had met and fallen in love with Marta Abba, the Milanese actress who joined his Arts Theatre in 1924. Plays written for Marta Abba tend to include a powerful, idealized central female figure, a part created especially for her talents, such as that of Tuda in *Diana and Tuda* (*Diana e la Tuda*) (1927) or of Marta in *The Wives' Friend* (*L'amica delle mogli*) of the same year. Quite apart from the biographical detail, these plays show

how Pirandello was able to write for a particular actress and a particular company, a sign of how far he had progressed from his earlier more literary type of theatre.

Pirandello's involvement in the physical practice of theatre making developed considerably through the 1920s. Sandro d'Amico and Jennifer Lorch have both shown how extremely receptive Pirandello must have been to the different exigencies that performance demanded from a text when he rewrote large parts of *Six Characters* after Pitoëff's production in 1923.[6] The 1925 edition of the play shows how far Pirandello had absorbed the lessons learned by the process of staging the first version. Later plays were written with performance needs in mind.

In 1925 Pirandello achieved his long standing ambition to set up an Arts Theatre based in Rome, a venture that involved him in both administrative and production work. Giudice summarizes Pirandello's contribution to Italian stage history as follows:

As a producer Pirandello is of particular importance in the meagre history of Italian stage production. He did not leave behind him a school or tradition, partly because he never actually specified his own ideas on production and acted purely on instinct. But his theatre was exemplary in Italy, owing to its repertoire and the rigour with which the actors were directed. Pirandello devoted himself to searching for a style of acting somewhere between the traditional Italian style, undisciplined, based on improvisation, but frequently brilliant, as in the case of individual actors like Tommaso Salvini, Zacconi, and Eleanora Duse, and the new school of European stage production, which had developed enormously from Meininger to Antoine's Théâtre Libre, the Deutsches Theatre in Berlin, and the

Moscow Arts Theatre, and which was based on infinitely painstaking preparation by the actors.

Allowing for Giudice's wild generalizations about theatre history, it is clear that Pirandello's concept of theatre involved rigid discipline and dedication on the part of the actors. Dario Niccodemi quotes him as saying:

> When I direct, the actors must study their parts and learn them by heart. They must study carefully, at home, on their own, in silence and meditation. And when they come on stage, they must not be actors any longer, they must be the characters in the play they are acting. That way they will have a reality in their own right that is absolute, not relative, it won't be the false truth of the stage but the positive, undeniable truth of life.[7]

And Pirandello is recorded as having fined two of his actors on one occasion for having 'acted in the way they did last night' after having undergone so much work. The links between Pirandello's method and Stanislawski's are so close that Pirandello began work at the Arts Theatre by giving his actors a lesson on the modern Russian theatre.

Pirandello's touring company that travelled extensively in Italy, Europe and South America, was dissolved in 1928, but he continued to write for the theatre, albeit with diminished success. He continued to travel, to attend rehearsals and to involve himself in the practical transfer of his plays to the stage, and in 1934 he directed Marta Abba and Ruggero Ruggeri in *La figlia di Jorio*, a play by d'Annunzio, the writer he had for so long disliked. It is important to remember the extent of Pirandello's involvement in the theatre, for again the tendency of a

21

more literary type of theatre criticism has tended to push this fact into the background. Pirandello was no closet dramatist; he had strong ideas about the theatre both in theory and practice.

As early as 1899 Pirandello had been expounding his ideas on the theatre in print. His essay 'Spoken Action' ('L'azione parlata') uses d'Annunzio as an example of a writer whose plays are too obviously devized by their author instead of emerging out of the characters and their situations. In his essay 'Theatre and Literature' ('Teatro e letteratura'), written in 1918, he develops this distinction further and argues for the special nature of a text that is neither badly written nor over-literary:

> The language will never be *common*; because it will belong to a given character in a given scene, it will belong to his personality, his passion, his role-playing.

Pirandello's belief in the specificity of theatre language and the high status of theatre as an art form is expressed with particular passion in his address to the Volta theatre Congress in 1934, one of his strongest statements and made just two years before his death:

> The Theatre cannot die.
> It is a form of life itself and we are all actors in it. If theatres were to be abolished or abandoned, theatre would continue unsuppressed in life; and the very nature of things would always be spectacle. In a time like our own, so full of contrasts and consequently so rich in dramatic material, amid such a ferment of passions and series of happenings that are overturning the whole life of nations, such a clash of events and instability of situations, with the need that is felt ever

more strongly to affirm to the bitter end some new certainty in the midst of such a tormented to-ing and fro-ing of doubts – to talk about the death of the theatre is truly a nonsense.

Pirandello the intellectual and the critics

The rhetoric of Pirandello's essay writing style sounds somewhat dated today and does not translate happily from Italian into English, but the sincerity of his beliefs comes through strongly enough. Since the extent of Pirandello's commitment to the theatre cannot be questioned, it is surprising that so much emphasis has been placed on the *ideas* implicit in his plays, rather than on the structures of the plays themselves and their place in theatre history. The explanation for this emphasis must derive, in large part, from the fundamental essay on Pirandello by the critic Adriano Tilgher in *Studi sul teatro contemporaneo* (*Studies in contemporary theatre*) in 1922. Tilgher's essay has continued to dominate critical response to Pirandello since its first appearance, and there is some evidence that Pirandello was himself influenced by the Neapolitan critic's assessment of his work.[8]

What Tilgher did was to explain Pirandello's work in terms of *antithesis*, which he declared to be 'the basic law of his art'. The fundamental motif of Pirandello's writing is seen as the eternal dualism between *Life*, on the one hand, that never ceases to move, and *Form* on the other, that seeks to fix Life and hold it:

All of modern philosophy, from Kant on, rises from this deep insight into the dualism between absolutely spontaneous Life, which in its perennial upsurge of freedom keeps creating the new, and the constructed

23

Forms or moulds which tend to imprison that upsurge, with the result that Life every time shatters those moulds to dissolve them and go beyond in its tireless creativity . . . To the eyes of an artist like Pirandello . . . reality will appear dramatic at its very roots, the essence of drama lying in the struggle between Life's primal nakedness and the garments or masks with which men must by all means insist on clothing it. *La vita nuda* (*Naked Life*), *Maschere nude* (*Naked Masks*). The very titles of his works are telling.

Art, then, is a kind of death since it freezes and fixes the unfixable. In *Diana and Tuda*, a play structured around this dilemma, Pirandello contrasts the life-energy of Tuda, the artist's model, with the death-bringing stasis of the statute that Sirio, the sculptor, is making of her. Unwilling to allow her to model for anyone else, Sirio marries her coldbloodedly, unable to respond to the love that she has for him. At the conclusion of the play Sirio is murdered by Giuncano, an older man, a failed artist, who loves Tuda unrequitedly and abhors what he sees as Sirio's blindness to Tuda's human potential. But the tragedy is not only one of unhappy love, for by this time Tuda herself has come to see the statue as more real and alive than she is herself. The statue has absorbed her life-energy and she is left with no possibility of realisation. Art has destroyed life and, in the process has become more real.

The statue or portrait metaphor recurs elsewhere in Pirandello's work (the portraits that apparently come to life in *Henry IV* or the portrait of Cia as she once was in *As You Desire Me* are among the most striking examples), as does the idea of art being to Life as a mirror is to the object it reflects. Both these images come together in theatre. Pirandello comes back again and again to the idea of the play itself as a means of demonstrating the continual dialectical process of the relationship between Life and Art. Theatre 'reproduces' or 'reflects' Life, it freezes events into the time span of the play; yet at the same time by its very nature it is itself part of the Life process, for the performance of one evening can never be exactly repeated again, it exists only while it is happening. Every performance of *Six Characters* is inevitably different from every other, yet what is being played is the fixed text written down, printed and therefore endurable. The theatre is the logical mode of expression for Pirandello's world vision. Tilgher saw this very clearly:

> As all of Pirandello's work tends to the theatre, so all his theatre tends to one perfect work totally expressing the Pirandellian intuition of life, like a pyramid tending to one point into which everything underneath may converge and be resolved.

Pirandello's vision of Life as a fluid process, as a kind of eternal river that can never be halted in any way is outlined in his essay 'On Humour' ('L'umorismo'), first published in 1908. Defining Life as 'flux' or flow, Pirandello argues that man creates a series of illusory devices to convince himself that the inexorable can be halted. These devices, or forms, through which man tries to achieve the consolidation of apparent stasis

> are the concepts and ideals by means of which we hope to give coherent enduring shape to all the fictions we create for ourselves, to the conditions and the state in which we tend to settle down and establish ourselves.

Art is only one such form; others include belief in social

25

position, idealism, the dream, all equally illusory since, as Pirandello puts it

> inside us, in what we call the soul, deep within that source of life in us, the flux continues imperceptibly. It seeps under the dykes we build, beyond the bounds we have imposed in an attempt to order our consciousness and construct a personality for ourselves.

At times these fictitious structures collapse, revealing the hollowness of their existence. Pirandello's fiction and plays continually revolve around the moment of exposure, the point at which the fictions collapse and the emptiness of human life is laid bare. Yet he is also at pains to point out that man has no alternative to the creation of illusory structures, for this is the only way to endow existence with any meaning:

> Each man patches up his mask as best he can – the mask he wears in public that is, but within each of us is another which often contradicts our external one. Nothing is true. Oh yes, the sea, a mountain, a rock, a blade of grass – these things are true. But man? Always wearing a mask, unwillingly, unwittingly – a mask of what he, in all good faith, believes himself to be: handsome, honourable, elegant, generous, unsuccessful, etc. . . . . He cannot ever stop posing and attitudinising over the most trifling events and details – even with himself. And he invents so much and creates so many parts for himself which he needs to believe in and take seriously.

Man creates a series of masks for himself, masks of identity that he assumes to fill various needs. In his novel

Introduction

One, No-one and a Hundred Thousand (*Uno, nessuno e centomila*) published in 1926, Pirandello explores the paradox of existence – a man is one person, in that the name conferred on him singles him out as such; many people in that he exists differently for everyone who knows him – as a son, a father, a friend, a professional figure, a tyrant, a genius, and so on; for millions of human beings that he passes in the street every day, he is nameless and without substance and for himself he is no-one at all. It is not too difficult to see the links with Sartre's notion of man existing through the reflected image of the Other. Pirandello's vision could be described as pre-Existentialist.

Identity, then, is a mask that man assumes for specific purposes. Many of Pirandello's plays revolve around the problem of the mask, where man may be in revolt against it, as in *The Pleasure of Honesty* (*Il piacere dell' onesta*), or forced to wear it, as in *Henry IV*, or consciously hiding behind it, as in *The Rules of the Game* (*Il giuoco delle parti*). The irony of Pirandello's concept of the mask, however, is that it does not hide an accessible truth. Once the mask is lifted, what remains is a series of other masks stretching into infinity because there can be no single true identity beneath. Just as the Life flow cannot be halted, truth cannot be established as identifiable.

Such a vision of human existence would be bleak indeed, if it were not for the way in which Pirandello expounds it. For Pirandello is not only a writer with a deeply pessimistic position, he is also an extremely funny writer. Pirandello's works are comic in the way that much of the silent cinema is comic. When Buster Keaton stands in bewilderment as his house falls down around him, audiences laugh, just as they laugh when Chaplin cooks his leather boots in a snowbound mountain cabin. Presented in another way, losing one's home and dying of starvation are deeply

27

tragic, but the framing devices used show these events in a comic light. Likewise with Pirandello, and although there are moments of extraordinary pity and terror in his theatre, there is also a strong sense of fun; some of the shifts of mood prefigure Brecht in their alienation effect. One such shift can be found at the end of *Tonight We Improvise*, when the tragic death of Mommina, incarcerated by her jealous husband, is followed by a squabble between the actors and the director in a sharp break of frame.

The great disservice that Tilgher did to Pirandello criticism was to overlook the comedy and to draw up his schematic analysis of the content–ideas of the works. Because of his stress on the ideas, he was led to the conclusion that Pirandello was an intensely intellectual dramatist, who used the theatre at times to expound a particular philosophical viewpoint. All too often, says Tilgher, the plays are 'the belaboured and gray scenic dressing of an abstract reflection or of a situational device which preceded and replaced dramatic vision'. He argues further that the dangers of a theatre such as Pirandello's are intrinsic to its very nature 'and the word *cerebralism* may sum them up, (meaning, this time, arid intellectualistic contrivance.)'. This judgement has been perpetuated through the decades since it was first made, and the stigma of 'cerebralism' still clings to Pirandello's theatre. It is curious that it should have endured so long, and curious also that the same stigma is not attached to many of those playwrights whom Pirandello supposedly prefigures. Critics do not say that Sartre, Brecht, Arrabal and Genet are overly difficult to understand, too 'intellectual' for the average theatre-goer or reader.

Pirandello's particular vision does, however, link him with one of the greatest minds of the century, in that his denial of an ideal of absolute truth brings him to a kind of philosophical theory of the relativity of things. The term 'relativity' used in relation to Pirandello describes a mode of awareness that basically refuses to accept the possibility of an exact definition of experience. Such a definition is impossible because:

(a) the perceiver is constantly changing;
(b) what is perceived is constantly changing;
(c) the means by which any perception is rendered is constantly changing.

Beneath this sense of fundamental impossibility is an equally powerful awareness of inter-relationships. Various critics have seized upon the parallels between Pirandello's relativism and the vision of the world exposed by Einstein's theory of relativity. Frederick May, for example, describes Pirandello as 'the exact interpreter of a world deriving its main acceptances from Einstein and from Freud'. Martin Esslin compares Pirandello's philosophy of personality directly with Einstein's theory of relativity, arguing that both have been responsible for a 'revolution in man's attitude to the world':

> Pirandello has transformed our attitude to human personality and the whole concept of *reality* in human relations by showing that the personality – character in stage terms – is not a fixed and static entity but an infinitely fluid, blurred and *relative* concept.[9]

This may seem to be an extravagant claim, but such has been the impact of Pirandello's work that the adjective *Pirandellian*, used to describe an absurd and ironically unsolvable situation has entered common usage. And nothing could be more Pirandellian than criticism's attempt to fix and define the extent of his contribution to

European culture. Using a favourite device of self-consciously referring to himself in one of his own plays, Pirandello's critics in *Each in His Own Way* argue about his work in a hilariously funny scene that simultaneously satirizes theatre critics and man's belief in absolute definitions:

THE IRRITATED SPECTATOR: Why can't one ever come to a first night of a Pirandello play without there being a fight?

THE GOOD-TEMPERED SPECTATOR: Let's hope nobody gets hurt.

SOMEONE WHO LIKES THE PLAY: It's a fine state of affairs though. When you come to other writers' plays you can settle down in your seat and be prepared to accept the illusion that the stage creates for you – if it manages to create one at all. But when you come to a Pirandello play you have to hang on to the arms of your seat with both hands – like this, and put your head down – like this – ready to butt back everything the writer tries to shove at you. You hear a word, any word, 'chair' for instance – oh God, hear that? he said 'chair'; he won't get away with that with me. Who knows what there is under that chair.

SOMEONE WHO DOESN'T LIKE THE PLAY: Yes, anything, everything – fine – except a bit of poetry that is.

OTHERS WHO DON'T LIKE THE PLAY: Exactly. And what we want is poetry.

SOMEONE ELSE WHO LIKES THE PLAY: If you want poetry, go and look under other people's chairs for it.

THOSE WHO DON'T LIKE THE PLAY: We've had enough of this spasmodic nihilism.

– And this pleasure he gets from denying things.

– Being negative just isn't constructive.

their staging is undistinguished compared to the fame of productions such as the Pitoëff or Rheinhardt *Six Characters*. *Each in His Own Way* was not performed in Italian for 37 years after its first staging, until the Teatro Carignano in Turin produced it in 1961. And although *Tonight We Improvise* has been staged more frequently, it is still not very well known outside Italy. One reason for the discrepancy in the number of productions of these two plays might be the sheer physical difficulties of the huge casts involved, while another explanation must surely lie in the relatively slight impact they made compared to the *succès de scandale* of *Six Characters*.

Pirandello's attack on the naturalist conventions of bourgeois theatre was not unique by any means, and his work should be seen in the context of a series of radical experiments in theatre practice. From the late nineteenth century onwards various alternatives to the conventions of the fourth wall were in evidence in theatres throughout Europe, and it would be fairer to see Pirandello's contribution as part of that wider movement than to claim, as some critics have done, that he occupies a pre-eminent position as an innovator. Landor McClintock, in his book that locates Pirandello within the wider context of Italian theatre, shows how far Pirandello was indebted to the *grottesco* school, typified by the plays of Luigi Chiarelli and Rosso di San Secondo whose works have more than a touch of Grand Guignol.[1] What distinguishes the plays of the trilogy, however, is the way in which Pirandello moves beyond the use of the stage as a means to attack either bourgeois drama or the popular highly rhetorical poetic drama of writers like D'Annunzio, to probe the whole nature of the convention of stage reality. He returns to the favoured device of the Elizabethan and Jacobean theatre, that of the play within a play, and challenges the conventional distinctions between appearance and reality by constantly switching levels. Erving Goffman, in *Frame Analysis (An Essay on the Organization of Experience)* notes that Pirandello uses three main formats for raising the issue of appearance and reality and tackling the question of frame:

> In one, illustrated by *Henry IV* and *The Rules of the Game*, the traditional respect for projected characters is sustained. In the second, *Six Characters in Search of an Author*, the conventional performer–character formula is attacked, but the attack stops at the stage line. In the third, this line between onstage and auditorium is breached in various ways.[2]

Each in His Own Way and *Tonight We Improvise* belong to this third category, when the security of the audience has been undermined to the extent that no-one knows whether he is sitting next to an actor disguised as a member of the audience or a 'real' person. In this way the theatrical experience mirrors Pirandello's vision of life as an indefinable and unstoppable process where security of perception is mere illusion.

'Six Characters in Search of an Author'

Six Characters is a play about the creation of a play, the two-fold process that takes place, first in the author's mind and then on the stage when the actors and director take over. It is as though Pirandello were seeking to present the notions of relativity of perception, language and communication in a suitable form, suitable insofar as it too is relative, subject to change and interpretation.

In the Preface to the play, added four years after the

first production and coinciding with the redrafting of large parts of the text, Pirandello explains the function of the Characters in relation to his own creative process. The play represents the coming together of art and life, of fixed form and moving vitality, but Pirandello has gone even further in his examination of this question, because he shows not only the problems of creating a play, but also the futility, since the play is just one more of the illusions that man builds to convince himself he *can* escape from the processes that shape his existence.

Six Characters is constructed on the three-act principle, with stage tricks being employed to blur the divisions into acts. The first section ends with the Characters and then the Actors leaving the stage, to take a natural break for twenty minutes, as it were, while the curtain remains up. The second section ends when the curtain is 'accidentally' let down by a stage hand, thus the formal division is maintained while at the same time the illusion of spontaneity is created. This highly disciplined technique that nevertheless creates the impression of being radically innovative led Pirandello to comment, in a letter to Ruggero Ruggeri shortly before his death in 1936, that the play was 'a true classic tragedy in which all the essential elements have been renewed', even though critics perceived it was 'the newest form of expression in theatre'.

The structure of the play defies straightforward plot summary, but the action can roughly be outlined as follows: a director rehearsing his actors for a performance of Pirandello's *The Rules of the Game* is interrupted by the arrival of six individuals (in Pitoëff's Paris production they arrived dramatically in a lift) who claim to be looking for an author to dramatize the story they have to tell. Through the first section of the play something of this story begins to unfold, as the Father and the Stepdaughter, locked in conflict with each other, attempt to win the director over to their respective points of view. The other Characters, the suffering Mother, the reluctant Son and the two silent small children remain on the fringes of this debate. What emerges as the discussion proceeds is that at some time in the past the Mother had gone to live with another man and had children by him, but whether this was because of the Father's cruelty or because of his generosity in wanting her to be happy elsewhere cannot be clarified. What is clear is that there is no communication between the Characters, whose multiple points of view prevent them from any understanding of the motivation of the others. The Father's speech on the futility of words is of central significance in this first section.

The Father's version of events, wherein he presents himself as a man motivated by love for the Mother and her children and by his belief in morality, is contrasted by the Stepdaughter's version. She depicts the Father as a moral coward and a disgusting human being, a man who followed her secretly to school as a child and who finally came face to face with her as a client of Madame Pace, the milliner-madame for whom the Stepdaughter had gone to work to help support the family after the death of her father. In section II Madame Pace appears, 'summoned up' by the Characters to enact the scene where Father meets Stepdaughter in the back room of the shop and, in a moment of high melodrama, the incestuous encounter is interrupted by the screams of the Mother.

In the third section the unhappy story moves to its tragic climax. The Father has brought the mother and her family back to his house again, a move opposed by the sullen, angry Son. The Mother tries in vain to win the Son over, since his rejection of her is unbearably painful. While her attention is focused on him the little girl drowns in the fountain in the garden and the small boy who has throughout the play been the object of the Stepdaughter's contempt shoots himself. The Stepdaughter flees from the house, leaving Father, Mother and Son locked in their irresolvable anguish.

Such are the apparent 'facts' of the Characters' story, and such was the distaste aroused by that story that audiences and critics were shocked and repelled by the squalor of it all when the play first appeared. But as with all Pirandello's plays the components of the plot are utilized for other ends. In *Six Characters* the details of the story emerge gradually as the Characters argue with each other and with the Director and Actors in scenes that are often extremely funny. The attempts in section II of the Actors to take on the roles of the Father and Stepdaughter illustrate the impossibility of art representing life, while the confusion that follows the apparent death of the children, when Actors and Director fail to agree on the reality of what they have seen, testifies to the power of art. The impossibility of resolving this conflict is summed up in the final words of the Director who curses them all for wasting his time in vain.

The cast list divides the persons appearing in the play into two separate groups: the Actors and the Director on the one hand and the Characters of the play in the making on the other. The Characters are listed simply by their positions vis-à-vis a family: the Father; the Mother; the Stepdaughter; the Son; the Boy; the Little Girl. There is one additional Character, Madame Pace, described in the cast list as *evocata* (summoned up), as indeed she is, later in the play. The division between the Characters and the others is continually reiterated over and over again, and from the moment of the Characters' first appearance the stage directions state that the separation must be presented in clear stage terms that the audience can grasp at once. Pirandello suggests that this may be effectively accomplished by means of lighting, by the contrast set up between the Actors already on the stage and the Characters entering through the auditorium, but feels that the best method of all is the use of masks for the Characters. The masks must be of a lightweight material and leave eyes, nostrils and mouth free. In this way, he explains, the meaning of the play will become clear:

> The Characters must not appear as *phantoms* but as *artificial realities* created out of unvarying fantasy. In this way they appear more real and consistent than the changeable naturalness of the Actors. Masks will help to give the impression of figures created through Art, each fixed unvaryingly in the expression of his or her basic feeling: *remorse* for the Father, *revenge* for the Stepdaughter, *disdain* for the Son, *grief* for the Mother.

In addition to the masks, directions are given for their clothes to be stiff and heavy, to give a statue-like appearance. Pirandello goes to great lengths in this later version of the play to ensure that there will be striking visual distinctions between the two groups and that the appearance of the Six Characters will intensify the idea of fixity and lack of fluid movement and change of expression. Pirandello's directions stress the *stylization* of the Characters' appearance, and only if this is borne in mind does the structure of the play make full sense. The mistake so often made in productions of *Six Characters* is to reverse those directions, to make the Characters appear 'natural' in contrast to the absurd over-acting of the Actors led by the poseur Director. The scenes where the Actors try to re-enact what the Characters have performed for them are bound to be very different in emphasis if the Actors are made to seem wooden and comically incompetent, and the Characters are presented naturalistically.

In addition to the details of the differing physical appearance of the two groups, the division between Characters and Actors is further emphasized by directions for their playing onstage. At the end of section I the two groups leave separately and when the curtain is raised at the start of section III they are seen sitting on opposite sides of the stage. In this way the breakdown of attempted communication of the first two sections is shown quite clearly. Actors and Characters have tried and failed to come together, and after the culminatory failure of the Madame Pace scene, the gulf continues to widen, until, in the final moments there is not even an attempt at communication between the two groups.

Throughout the play the Director and the Characters clash on two fundamental issues: the problem of defining the limitations of theatre and the distinction between rehearsing and living a scene. This clash of views reaches its climax in section II when Madame Pace 'materializes' on stage. As the Characters prepare for their scene in the room at the back of her shop, the Director calls in the Prompter to write down everything that is said so that it can be used later. The prompter's duty has been reversed, his function now is to turn life into a written text instead of reminding actors of their lines from a predetermined script. Moreover, the gap between the life script and the theatre script involves the need for certain conventions of art to be followed. So when the Stepdaughter reminds the Director that the dress the Father tried to make her take off was black because she was still in mourning, the Director tries to dismiss her, on the grounds that this would be too much for the public to take. The Stepdaughter argues back:

> THE STEPDAUGHTER: But it's the truth.
> THE DIRECTOR: What truth, for God's sake? This is the theatre. – We can only take so much truth here.

Only certain things are performable in the theatre, and the Director insists that he is not concerned with life as it happened, but with life as it can be presented to the public within the package called theatre. The play returns again and again to a discussion of this problem, to the distinction between the Characters' insistence on reproducing the truth of their story and the Director's attempts to fit the details they give him into a suitable frame, regardless of whether or not he makes any alterations. The keyword *prova* (*rehearsal*) recurs throughout the play and is used with greatest frequency in section II where, as the following example demonstrates, the word shows up the abyss between the two groups gathered on stage for totally different purposes:

> THE DIRECTOR: Right now we're going to try and have a rehearsal. They'll do it. (*Pointing to the Actors*)
> THE FATHER: (*stunned, as if he had just dropped onto the stage from nowhere*) We are? I'm sorry, but what do you mean by a rehearsal?
> THE DIRECTOR: I mean a rehearsal – a rehearsal for them. (*Pointing to the Actors*)
> THE FATHER: But if we're the characters . . . .
> THE DIRECTOR: OK fine, you're the 'characters', but here, friend, characters don't act. Actors do the acting. Characters stay there (*pointing to the Prompter*) in the script.

So the conflict goes on: Madame Pace's accent proves so amusing to the Actors that the Director tells her to keep on using it, because it will have certain effect, and the Stepdaughter counters by saying that this is how she speaks in life. At the end of section II and the beginning of the next section, the Director talks about splitting the Characters' story into 'Acts' and sees the Mother's interruption of the scene between the Father and the Stepdaughter as an 'effective' climax to his Act I. In section III, the Director arranges a garden, and again there is a clash between what he expects and what the Characters intend to do. The Son and Mother maintain that they cannot be in the garden because their scene takes place in his room, but the Director dismisses this as irrelevant. It is at this point that the Son turns and attacks him, in a manner reminiscent of the Actors' revolt against Hinkfuss in *Tonight We Improvise*:

> Don't you understand yet that you can't do this play? We're not inside you at all and your actors are just looking at us from the outside.

Communication between the Characters and the Director proves to be impossible. The Father tries to explain the contrast between the life of a Character, fixed in 'unchangeable reality' and the life of someone like the Director whose reality is part of a fluid process that time can alter and distort, but the Director cannot understand. He keeps insisting on the importance of the rules of theatre, refusing to consider anything that cannot be explained in his terms.

Throughout the play he is concerned with *rehearsing*, firstly with his Actors and then, after the arrival of the Characters, with their story. The bare stage and the technicians who come and go, the actors in brightly coloured everyday clothes and the Director's constant interruptions all serve as a visual reminder to the audience of the 'rehearsal' in progress. The Director agrees to the Father's request for an opportunity to present their drama, but sees the request almost as a joke – and when he calls together the Actors and Technicians to watch two Characters play their scenes, he reiterates the word *prova*. After the Madame Pace scene, the Actors take over the 'rehearse' what they have just witnessed, except that now, of course, the situation is changed and what was life is presented as art in a contrived form. The Director perceives the Characters' scenes as 'rehearsals', but as they continue to insist, what they are enacting is their life, their reality. When the Actors try to repeat the same scene it is different, and the Father and Stepdaughter are appalled at seeing themselves reflected in the inadequate mirror provided by the Actors playing the roles.

But the word *prova* in Italian has more than one meaning. It can be 'rehearsal' or 'trial' and it can also be the third person singular, present indicative, of the verb *provare* (to feel, experience). The same sounding word can, in different contexts, have an opposite meaning. For the Characters, *provare* has the significance of 'feeling' and reinforces the suffering they have come to present, whereas for the Director, suffering is only apparent in its outward manifestations that have to be rehearsed for the right effect. Such a distinction in terms is lost when the play is read or seen in English.

Another key word that recurs through the play is *immaginare* (to imagine). In section I, which is largely dominated by the Father, the phrase *Lei s'immagini* (Just imagine) is used repeatedly. As the Characters try to build a background to their story, they have to keep appealing to the Director and the Actors to 'imagine' certain situations, in the same way that all theatre requires an effort of imagination on the part of an audience. The Characters' story is compressed into two scenes: the encounter between the Father and Stepdaughter in Madame Pace's shop and the death of the children in the garden. The rest of the story has to be imagined, and the conflicting versions return again to the problem of the relativity of perception and interpretation. The Father tries to talk about this problem in section I:

> The drama for me is all here, sir: in the awareness I have that though each one of us thinks he's uniquely consistent, you see, even believes it, it isn't true. Everyone is many people, sir, many people according to all the possibilities of being that are in all of us. We're one person here, another person with somebody else – completely different. Yet all the time we have the illusion of being the same for everybody and of being that one person we think we are in everything we do. It's just not true. And we come to realize that when something terrible happens and because of one thing we do we suddenly find ourselves hooked and hanging in the air, so to speak. What I mean is, we can see that not every bit of ourselves is involved in that one action and so it would be a wicked injustice to judge us by that action alone, to keep us hooked up and suspended on a gallows for our whole lifetime, as if our existence itself were summed up in that one action.

The Father protests that the Stepdaughter has judged and condemned him by what he describes as 'one fleeting shameful moment' in his life. He continues to argue that he is a decent, moral man in spite of his visit to Madame

Pace's and resents the way in which the Stepdaughter has allowed that one incident to colour her view of him as a human being. But there is another dimension to the Father's speech: in his position as a Character created by an author but part of an incompleted story, his protest is against the irony that has condemned him to such fixity, with no additional scenes that might alter the balance in any way.

Early in section 1, the Father talks about the uselessness of words as a means of communication, although he constantly tries to 'intellectualize' the situation, and this section contains many long, didactic monologues spoken by the Father. He and the Stepdaughter are the most articulate of the Characters because, as the Prologue explains, they are the most complete, 'the most alive, most fully rounded'. The Mother, however, is the 'resigned victim', whilst the children 'have hardly any consistency at all except barely in their appearance and have to be led on by the hand'. The Son, who is conceived on yet another level, is described as 'reluctant, and right from the start, when the Father tries to include him with the others he declares that he has nothing to do with the other Characters' search for an author.

The Son's first entry shows his resentment and the positioning of the Characters in their first meeting with the Director emphasizes this feeling in strong visual terms. The Stepdaughter enters in a rush, arriving first on stage, closely followed by the Father, while the Mother and children wait halfway. The Son alone makes no attempt to join the others, and is thus immediately isolated, while his attitude is seen to be very different from that of the other characters. As the Characters unfold their story the Son keeps trying to stay out of it all, denying his involvement almost to the end. Yet when told to go by the Stepdaughter he finds that he cannot; the stage directions describe him as 'bound by an almost occult power'. The Stepdaughter exults – 'He has to stay here, he's forced to, he's bound to the chain forever.' The Son, whether he likes it or not, was created as part of the family and *must* share in their tragedy. There can be no escape from what is predetermined and as a Character he has no choice but to stay. On another level, he is tied to the stage because as an actor his world begins when he steps out in front of the audience and ends when he leaves the stage, since once an actor is no longer on stage as part of the play he no longer exists for the audience. He is compelled to live out his part on stage because once he leaves it he is nothing. On a third level, the Son represents man condemned to be alive. If the stage mirrors life and the actor is compelled to be on that stage in order to exist, so mankind is compelled to go on living in order to be. The metaphor of the stage as life is a constant undercurrent in this play and the Six Characters with their fixed masks bring a life to the stage that the conscious imitations of the Actors can never have. The senselessness of the artificial stage world, and of life itself that brings so much pain, together with the way in which the one mirrors the other, recalls the most intense moments of Shakespearean tragedy. The notion of man condemned to life reflected in the actor condemned to appear within the confines of the stage is reiterated in increasingly clear terms in later twentieth-century drama. With Pirandello the problem is discussed within the limits of a conventional dramatic framework, because *Six Characters* is made to fit the three-act mould. Later in *Each in His Own Way* and *Tonight We Improvise* the basic three-act structure is replaced by something less rigid. In *Six Characters* the Son's helplessness may be seen as a foretaste of the situation in which Beckett's tramps find themselves. It is a situation where action is futile and provides no solution, and it is possible to see Beckett's ultimate concept of the 'non-play' as an extension of Pirandello's portrayal of the reluctant actor. An actor who desires not to appear may be parallel to a man contemplating suicide – once the step has been taken and the suicide succeeds, its stage equivalent must be the 'non-play' where there are no actors at all, nothing but the bare stage without movement or sound, the final reaches of pessimism that also mean the end of drama.

But there is still a long gap between Pirandello and, for example, Beckett's *Breath* (which may be described as a 'non-play' in so far as there is no visual action). The Son cannot leave the stage, resigns himself and becomes, finally, the only Character able to speak and relate unequivocally what he saw:

the boy, the boy just standing there looking crazy, staring at his little sister drowned in the pond ....

The Son recounts the final climax, which is completed by the revolver shot and the Mother's screams. True to his original stated intentions, he has refused to participate in any 'scenes', but being bound to the family and to the stage he must play his part in the tragedy. He has no freedom to leave, he can only choose not to speak and at the end even this choice is denied him as he becomes the narrator, in a half conscious way 'slowly, staring straight ahead'. At this point, he has a function similar to that of the Chorus in Greek tragedy, a part of the total visual play and yet a non-performer in the actions of the plot.

The Son's inability to leave the stage is another example of the 'magic' power the theatre can have. In the final scene, the stage directions refer specifically to this power, when the Stepdaughter calls her Mother 'as though pulling her forward by some magic power'. The Characters themselves in their masks and costumes clash with the Actors and these clashes are a constant reminder of the contrast between the 'magical' world of the theatre and the world outside its boundaries. Most crucial of all scenes in this respect is the one where Madame Pace is 'summoned up' in section II.

In the scene where Madame Pace appears, illusion and reality are deliberately blurred by the author. The Director has been busily trying to set up a scene to resemble the interior described by the Characters when he realizes that Madame Pace is not with them. The Father explains that she may not be there at that moment but is alive nevertheless. He then borrows the hats and coats of some of the Actors and hangs them on the racks provided, 'on show', to draw Madame Pace to the stage. When Madame Pace appears, the stage directions show the terror of the Actors and Director at the 'witchcraft' that has brought about her sudden arrival. The Actors then protest, saying that some kind of trick must have been played on them. They are incapable of seeing her entry in stage terms and therefore are terrified by what appears to be an illogical occurrence of life. The Actors, watching the scene, believe that they *are* watching a rehearsal, so they study the Characters with the intention of later repeating what they have seen. The hats and coats are props, and the Young Actress interrupts to remind Characters and audience alike of this fact. But on another level they are not props, they are indeed the hats belonging to Madame Pace, an intrinsic part of her life as created by the author who outlined the Characters' story. Imagination has created the special reality of theatre. In the final scene, the fact of the child's drowning is laid down in the story outlined by the author and is quite unrelated to whether the fountain we see is a fake and was carried on by a stagehand. In so far as the stage represents life and in so far as the Characters have a tragic story to unfold and live out, the two children must die and, as the Father cries in his last desperate speech, it is no fiction for them but reality.

Six Characters presents the audience with an 'under-play', with the tools, the executors and the characters for a play, leaving the interpretation to the relative understanding of the audience. But at the same time it is a play that an audience goes to watch performed in a theatre. Pirandello has created a play about the processes of artistic creation, a study of the relativity of form enclosed within a formal framework. It is therefore not only a play that contains within it another play, it is a play about the nature of the play constructed on a Chinese box principle, where the answering of one question merely opens the lid to another.

'Each in His Own Way'

Each in His Own Way has frequently been regarded as the odd one out of the trilogy, the weak link, where Pirandello becomes over-involved in his attempts to fragment the traditional structure of the play. Yet a close examination of this play shows that, far from being over-long and muddled, *Each in His Own Way* is carefully contrived, and is as precisely structured as any of Pirandello's three-act plays.

The play is divided into four sections: two acts, in which the main story line is developed, and two 'Choral Intermezzi', in which groups of theatre critics and members of the public debate first the effectiveness and then the veracity of what they have seen in the previous act. The third act does not take place because the play is interrupted by Amalia Moreno, the outraged member of the audience who claims that the play is based on her life and is an insult that is more than she can stand. In the second Intermezzo, Amalia Moreno goes backstage and slaps the leading lady; the resulting public scene forces the management to cancel the rest of the performance.

Amalia Moreno's attack has been carefully prepared even before the action onstage begins. Pirandello's directions give precise details for the scene that is to be improvized in the foyer of the theatre as the audience is assembling. Amalia Moreno with a group of friends is to be seen arguing, in a state of some distress, insisting that she wants to go in and see the performance:

> This improvised scene, exactly like life, should start a few minutes before the performance is scheduled to begin and should last right up to the moment when the bell is rung in the auditorium, amid the surprise, curiosity and probably also apprehensiveness of the real audience who are moving into the theatre.

In this way Pirandello cuts through the convention of the time-span of a performance. *Each in His Own Way* may be said to begin with this improvized scene, this happening in the theatre foyer that some members of the audience will see, rather than with the raising of the curtain. This represents a far more radical attempt to challenge stage reality than anything in *Six Characters.* As the play progresses, it switches in and out of the two sequences in a way that prevents the audience from settling down to follow a unified course of action. Moreover, Acts I and II are made up of a series of scenes involving two or three characters at a time. Instead of continuous action, what we see is a sequence of separate sections welded together, giving an almost cinematic effect and speeding up the overall pace. In this way the structure reflects the leit-motif of the play: the fragmentary nature of life itself and man's vain search for some kind of fixed point of reference.

The plot line of the two acts is typical of Pirandello in its ironic twists and turns. Act I opens in the palatial home of Donna Livia Palegari who is giving a party, with two short scenes in which guests are overheard, as it were, in the midst of private conversations. These opening scenes provide an introduction to what is to follow, concerned as they are with problems of talking and listening, with the gap between what is said and what is understood. Luigi Squarzina, who directed the revival of *Each in His Own Way* in Genoa in 1961, claims that these opening scenes are 'one of the most modern things the theatre of this century has to offer', since they represent an author parodying his own poetics. The opening scenes also introduce the basic metaphor of the play, that of *confession*. Donna Livia's drawing room is described in the stage directions as looking like a church, and the farcical scenes of the first act are played out against this para-religious background.

Confession represents a particular type of communication. It involves a three-part process: one must first look into oneself to make a decision on what is to be confessed, then comes the verbalization in the act of confession itself and finally there is the return process of penance and absolution. What happens in *Each in His Own Way* is that absolution is never given, while different kinds of confession take place as characters give in to an overwhelming need to talk to and be heard by others.

After the opening discussions, the character of Diego Cinci is introduced. At first appearance he is an example of the recurring figure of the cynical observer, typified by

Laudisi in *Right You Are*, but as the play progresses he too is seen as someone who suffers and who cannot find absolution. No-one is exempted in this play, no-one is permitted to stand on the sidelines and be uninvolved in the painful processes of living. Donna Livia interrogates Diego Cinci about her son, Doro. She is convinced that he is in love with Delia Morello, a woman whose reputation is scandalous and whose previous lover is said to have committed suicide on account of her. It appears that Doro defended Delia Morello the night before in an argument with Francesco Savio, his friend, who maintained that she was guilty of causing her lover's death. Doro enters and declares himself ready to change his mind if necessary, but when Francesco Savio comes to apologize and announces that he too has changed his mind, Doro loses his temper and insults him. At this ludicrous point Delia Morello herself arrives, to thank Doro for having defended her honour. She insists that he has fully understood her point of view, and explains how she came to steal her present lover, Michele Rocca, away from his fiancée, the dead man's sister, out of pure selflessness, in an attempt to prevent him from making a disastrous marriage. Doro is delighted to hear his original interpretation vindicated and tells Delia the details of Francesco Savio's counter-argument. Delia then changes tack completely and suggests that this might indeed be the truth. The act ends with Donna Livia rushing onstage to ask whether it is true that Doro has insulted Savio and will be challenged to a duel.

In Act II the action takes place in Francesco Savio's house. He is preparing to fight the duel with Doro and is interrupted by Diego Cinci, come to try and point out the absurdity of what has happened, which he does in a language that is heavily derived from Pirandello's essay 'On Humour'. They are interrupted by Michele Rocca, come to offer yet another version of the story: that he deliberately became Delia's lover following a pact between himself and the dead man. His action, he claims, was intended to prove Delia's worthlessness to her fiancé, who would then abandon her, but instead he killed himself. The confusion is now at its height – there are so many versions of the Delia Morello story that any pretence at establishing the 'truth' has become ridiculous, and the duel of honour totally meaningless. All discussion comes to a halt when Delia Morello arrives and she and Rocca meet. Their carefully maintained arguments collapse and they are overwhelmed by a tide of mutual passion. The act ends with Francesco's comment that they are both mad and Diego's retort 'Because you don't look at yourself!'

Such a plot is similar to many others in Pirandello's stories and plays, but what distinguishes *Each in His Own Way* is the down-grading of the tradition of plot structuring. At the end of Act I, in the first Intermezzo, the Spectators argue over the merits of what they have seen, over whether the play is *à clef*, over what they think Pirandello is trying to do. Amalia Moreno, increasingly hysterical, insists on staying for the second act, but in the second Intermezzo she goes to pieces, claiming to have seen herself onstage portrayed as Delia Morello. She is restrained by Nuti, her lover, with whom she enacts a scene so similar to that which has just taken place between Rocca and Delia that members of the public comment that they are re-enacting it. Art has anticipated life, and life appears as a pale copy.

Both sections of *Each in His Own Way* deal with the concept of infinite change as perceived through the inadequacy of language as a means of communication. The crises of the Delia Morello plot occur because of the confusion caused when characters try to reach each other through speech and fail, speech being a way of trying to establish order out of the confusion of half-formed thoughts. 'Life,' says Pirandello in the essay 'On Humour', 'is a continuous flux that we keep trying to halt and fix in stable, determined forms within us and around us.' With words man tries to shape his unshapable thoughts and control the world in which he moves, but the unforeseen – the moment of passion, the interruption of the play – can always destroy his carefully built illusion of security.

The keywords of the play are three verbs: *pensare* (to think), *sapere* (to know) and *dire* (to say), all of which are part of the process of confession. From the start a pattern is established of question and answer units, where characters in both the Delia Morello plot and the Intermezzi ask for certitude that they never receive. In the opening scene of Act I the Old Family Friend is forced to fend off the insistent questioning of the rather aggressive Young Man, and the duel becomes the symbol of the verbal parrying and sidestepping, apparent from this first scene, that runs throughout. Speech is a weapon that can be used to attack and to defend, and the play is built around the series of verbal battles in both Acts and Intermezzi. The acts divide into encounters between characters. In the first act alone there are ten such encounters. In the Intermezzi, the idea of verbal battle is even more pronounced and is reinforced by the stage directions. In the general *mêlée* of the first Intermezzo the Critics in Favour of the Play and those Against the Play form separate groups and insult each other, while the second Intermezzo opens with confusion and shouting as reported accounts of Amalia Moreno's attack on the Leading Lady are exchanged.

When Amalia slaps the Leading Lady, a number of

conflicts within the play run together. The verbal battles, the duel that never takes place, the struggle that Diego has with his guilty memories over his mother's death are all manifestations of the forces of movement and change that make up life. The characters in both parts of *Each in His Own Way* are engaged in a struggle of which they are mainly unaware: the struggle to create and maintain an illusory shell of security in which to exist. At the same time Amalia's attack focuses attention on another aspect of the fixity–motion conflict: the contrast between the unpredictableness of life and the ordered frame of art. The Father of *Six Characters* expresses his horror of this when he tries to explain that characters are fixed forever in their roles and cannot die; when Amalia cries out that she has seen herself on stage she expresses horror at 'seeing myself there performing that action'. Her horror is not only because she feels insulted by a play that seems to be based on her own life, but because she feels that the play has fixed her in a gesture she could not contemplate in reality. The irony, of course, is that she *does* the very thing she has been protesting about – she throws herself into Nuti's arms, overwhelmed by passion in the same way as Delia Morello throws herself into the arms of Michele Rocca. The difference is that the one gesture is momentary, whilst the other can be repeated whenever the play is staged. By a further irony, such a distinction is presented to us within the fixed frame of a play.

Each in His Own Way is a highly complex play, and the construction serves to reinforce the thematic components. The Intermezzi repeat and strengthen concepts introduced in the two acts and vice versa, besides providing a means of balancing the tragic and comic elements. Significantly, the Intermezzi are described as 'choral'; the many voices of the Spectators with their changeable opinions do serve as a kind of chorus. The Spectators, described in the cast list as *momentanei* (occasional characters) as opposed to the characters of the Delia Morello plot who are described as *fissati* (permanently fixed), act as both a further reinforcement of the infinite variety concept, and are vehicles for satirizing the absurdities of defining 'artistic taste'. As with *Tonight We Improvise*, this play is a sharp attack on theatre criticism. The characters of the Intermezzi are caricatures, rigid embodiments of their own views. In the cast list they are defined by those views under headings such as: The Peaceable Spectator, the Angry Spectator, Those in Favour, Those Against, A Literary Man Who is Above Writing, An Old Failed Author and so forth. The futility of the search for the true explanation of the Delia Morello story is mirrored in the futility of the critics' attempts to assess and categorize what they have seen. Like *Right Your Are (If You Think So)* the title sums up the impossibility of these searches for the absolute. There can be no ultimate conclusion, and each person will think, feel and respond in his or her own way even though he may fail to see that multiple opinions are relative. The arbitrariness of life is mirrored in the arbitrariness of what the characters say.

Each in His Own Way swings violently from farcical comedy to sombre moments such as Diego's reflections on his mother's death. These changes of mood are also carefully contrived, to avoid the possibility of the play being defined in any single way. The concept of relative opinion that underlies both sections of the play is presented on the surface as comedy. The witticisms, the fast pace, the head-spinning changes of mind, the satire on theatre criticism, the grotesque characters, the lack of any final tragic climax, all framed by the comic confusion with which the action begins and ends serve to make what must be one of Pirandello's funniest plays. But at the same time, beneath that comic front is a profoundly dark underlay. The characters cannot communicate with one another, they are tormented by self-doubt and the Delia Morello play is full of references to death. As Diego Cinci explains in Act II, death, the final stasis, is not only unavoidable, it is also what everyone is seeking because it is the ultimate point of fixity and security. Yet there is no way even of defining death, it can only be looked at in the same way as we might watch a play. Suddenly moved to talk about his mother's death, Diego Cinci tells Donna Livia how he sat at the dying woman's bedside and became so involved in watching an insect try to escape from a glass of water into which it had fallen that he watched its death instead of hers. He tells this story early in Act I, as a kind of parable that serves two purposes. For Donna Livia the story is meant to show her that her own supposed suffering over whether Doro is in love with Delia is relatively insignificant. It also illustrates how mankind is only capable of determining the importance of events when they are past and beyond control. The accidental fate that made the insect fall in front of Diego distracted him from the most terrible and most final of all human spectacles: death. Unable to turn back the clock, he is haunted by the memory of what he sees as his neglect of his dying mother. His torment is the 'horror' felt by Amalia Moreno when she sees herself; it is the endless repetition of a terrifying moment in time reproduced in the mind, the theatre of the soul.

Later in Act I Diego returns again to his memory of that deathbed, recalling how his mother's breathing had stopped and how, for a brief instant, he had thought she was dead. Death, at that point, was perceived as a relief from suffering and was what Diego most desired. This second reference to his mother's death serves also as a parable; although death may be the way out of a painful existence, man is compelled by his being to go on enduring that pain.

Each in His Own Way is therefore profoundly pessimistic, since it demonstrates the impossibility of a way out for man, condemned to live with others and unable to communicate with them. The only final escape from life is the sterile immobility of death, where all is silence. But the structure of the play deliberately belies the impact of that pessimism; because of its constantly changing perspectives it could be described, with Pound's permission, as 'a broken bundle of mirrors'. Discussing his staging of the play – he used a revolving stage to swing from the Delia Morello sets to the Intermezzi – Squarzina expresses his aim to move away from Tilgher's narrow art–life dichotomy:

> By moving continuously from identification to alienation and back to identification again, we presented Pirandello's reality as a playing with mirrors, as I think Pirandello really wanted it to be, but never as a Manichean dichotomy of reality! Like *a* and *b*, black and white – never.[3]

Squarzina also defends his decision to stage this play that one critic had described as made up of a 'mountain of irrelevances', by maintaining that *Each in His Own Way* is one of Pirandello's major works – 'I thought I could see in it a great Pirandello – the equal of Joyce, Kafka and Musil'. While such claims can often be counter-productive, Squarzina does make a strong case for a re-evaluation of the play as representative of a further stage in Pirandello's development as a writer for the theatre. In this second play of the theatre trilogy (put together by Pirandello himself in a single volume in 1933), Pirandello has gone even further in destroying the fiction of stage reality. In the third play, *Tonight We Improvise* he was to go on to make a play about the very processes of playing.

'Tonight We Improvise'

Tonight We Improvise is the most radical example of Pirandello's attempts to write a play about theatre, although its scope and complexity have worked against its frequent staging. The play explores the question of the meaning of theatre and examines the roles of playwright, director, actors and audience, while at the same time using this exploration as a metaphor for considering the function of art in life and the tension that exists between the refining process of the one and the limitless motion of the other. Above all, *Tonight We Improvise* is a play about the relativity of freedom (the keywords are *liberazione*, *liberare*, *libero* – freedom, to release, free) in both art and life, for just as actors are doomed to the confines of the stage in order to have any being, so human beings are doomed to the spatial and temporal limits of their own life span. Freedom is therefore impossible, and all the escape routes such as dreams, imagination, illusion lead to dead ends.

The complex structure of the play makes it difficult to summarize. Again, as with the other plays in the trilogy, Pirandello uses framing devices: a director, Hinkfuss, tries to organize his actors to perform a play. There is to be no fixed script, the actors are to improvize their lines, and right from the start it is obvious that the actors are unhappy with the whole idea. Much of the comedy in the play comes from the clashes between Hinkfuss and the actors, who finally succeed in throwing him out only to have him reappear to claim the credit at the end. Hinkfuss as a director is pompous, wordy, arrogant and overly ambitious; he has been seen as Pirandello's satire on the exaggerated power enjoyed by such directors as Pitoëff and Reinhardt. Hinkfuss clearly has contempt for his actors, whom he attempts to control like so many puppets, and even greater contempt for his audiences, whom he regards as stupid and easily impressed. But when the actors unite to get rid of him, they point out in no uncertain terms that his presence is useless:

> THE LEADING ACTOR: Real theatre!
>
> THE COMIC ACTOR: What you chuck away every night! Your idea of theatre is just giving people something flashy to look at.
>
> THE CHARACTER ACTRESS: When you live out a feeling, that's real theatre; then all you need is the odd prop.
>
> THE LEADING LADY: You can't play around with feelings.
>
> THE LEADING ACTOR: You can only juggle everything for effects if you're dealing with petty comedies.
>
> ALL THE OTHERS: Get out.
>
> DR. HINKFUSS: I am your director.
>
> THE LEADING ACTOR: Life can't be directed by anyone when it's coming into being.

In this central scene we see the strength of Pirandello's views on theatre, repeatedly expressed in his theoretical writings. Theatre, he argues, through the Actors, is not artificially created great effects, it is a quasi-mystical moment of fusion between life and the play. As the play develops the actor lives his part for the period of time that it takes for the play to run its course. It is not too difficult to see the links between Pirandello's idea of life for a character and Stanislawski's notion of the actor absorbing the role he plays, while his attack on the exaggerations of spectacle theatre point to his sympathy for a theatre of flesh and blood rather than a theatre of high technique. When Hinkfuss sets the scene for the Sicilian drama that his actors are to play, he devises a 'synthetic representation' of Sicily, with a religious procession, national dress, dozens of people and so forth, and later in the play he creates an airfield, because one of the characters is supposed to be an air force officer. The absurdity and irrelevance of such lavish stage effects are clearly apparent, and contrast vividly with the moment when the actress playing Mommina builds an illusory room around herself on stage:

> *The Leading Lady, left alone between the three bare walls of her prison which have been erected in the darkness while she was being dressed and made up, comes forward to touch them with her forehead; first the right hand wall, then the back wall, then the left. Each time her forehead touches the wall, it is lit up for a second by a sharp beam of light, like a cold lightening flash, then disappears again in the darkness.*
> THE LEADING LADY: (*speaking with heavy rhythms, with growing intensity, touching the three walls with her forehead like a maddened beast in a cage*) This is a wall. – This is a wall. – This is a wall.

Nothing else is needed to create an impression of pain and imprisonment, and the illusion of the reality of that pain will be maintained by the communication between actress and audience.

Hinkfuss is the personification of everything that Pirandello sees as negative in theatre, he is an anti-theatre force. In the opening scene Hinkfuss appears to explain to the audience (and there are 'plants' in the audience, who argue amongst themselves and with Hinkfuss, thus blurring the lines between stage and auditorium as the place where the action of the play occurs) what he means by improvization. *My* actors, as he calls them, have been given a basic story outline and will work from that. In this way, he claims, he has eliminated the need for an author. The actors are therefore freed from the constraints of both author and script.

This freedom, however, is a sham, since the existence of a story outline is already a limitation and since Hinkfuss intends to make the actors follow his every order. As the play proceeds, we can see how absurdly restricting Hinkfuss' idea of freedom is, for Hinkfuss is a believer in absolute values and rules and tries to force everything and everyone into prefixed moulds. The actors' revolt against him is therefore a revolt both against the tyranny of rigid beliefs, and against his particular idea of theatre.

The first stage of revolt against Hinkfuss introduces a number of issues that are dealt with increasingly as the play proceeds. When we first see the actors, they immediately begin to argue over their right to be able to lose themselves in the personalities of the roles they are playing. Hinkfuss explains that theatre relies on coexistence – the director needs actors and technicians as living tools with which to make his play, while the actors need the framework he creates for them – but he fails to see how the relationship between actor and role can exist without him.

In the second stage of revolt the actors threaten to leave the stage altogether and thus deprive Hinkfuss of his raw material. Then they order Hinkfuss to leave, and when he protests they tell him what he has done. By allowing the actors to improvize, and take over the personalities of the characters he wanted them to represent, Hinkfuss has given life to a whole new group of persons and he has become superfluous. The Leading Man acknowledges that they are all trapped by the existence of an audience ('here is the public that can't be sent away'), but goes on to say that they will continue not as actors but as characters presenting their story for the judgement of others. This is the reverse of the situation presented in *Six Characters*, where the Characters lived on a level impossible for the Actors. Here the Actors take over and become the characters for a short time.

In the clash between Hinkfuss and the actors, we see exemplified the clash between the absolute and the relative. Hinkfuss wants to impose order even on improvization, everything must be defined and conform to his vision. The actors demand the freedom to allow chance impressions and unprogrammed action to happen without a predetermined pattern: that is, they demand to bring characters to life. But when, at the end of the play, Hinkfuss reappears to claim the credit, and we hear that he has been secretly controlling the lighting effects, we can see that the actors have only a very limited kind of freedom, restricted by the stage, the audience and above all by the fact that they are reproducing other lives. Mommina the character dies, but the Leading Lady does not. The play is limited in time, but the actors' lives go on after it has ended. As the Old Comic Actor sums up the vital difference between acting, even improvized acting, and living: acting can only exist up to a point, reality on stage is limited: 'no-one can expect an actor to kick the bucket every night'. The actor can only reproduce reality within the limits set by theatre. Once an actor feels real pain or actually dies, he is no longer acting. The actors' revolt cannot ultimately succeed, because they demand the freedom of life within the constrictions of theatre and this is impossible. At the same time, Pirandello is using the theatre, as he so often does, as a metaphor for life. Ultimate freedom, whether to leave the stage or to leave life through death, is negation.

Tonight We Improvise is not tied to a stage, but moves round the theatre. Action takes place on the stage, in the lobby, in a box in the auditorium and among the audience. Scene i consists of an exchange between Hinkfuss and some Spectators, following the argument among these false Spectators about whether the play has actually begun or not. Indeed, the first words to be heard are 'What's going on?' as people try to understand whether they are hearing sounds of an argument coming from behind the scenes or whether this is an intentional part of the action. In this first scene the question of the freedom of the audience is explored, for the placing of false Spectators creates doubts as to whether the person one is sitting next to is an actor or not. Pirandello deliberately tries to involve the audience on a level that goes beyond the question of their response to what they see taking place on stage. In Act I, for example, the stage directions call for the 'Spectators' in all parts of the house to start clapping, with the rider 'they will stop at once if the real public don't catch on and follow suit', while during the Intermission the play continues both on stage and out in the theatre lobby in two distinct sequences. The audience are thus made an active part of the theatre event, a further indication of how much Pirandello despised Hinkfuss' notion of the audience as a passive body that could be manipulated by clever stage tricks.

The story line that Hinkfuss has chosen for his actors to

follow is, he tells us, taken from a written text. It is a Sicilian story, revolving around the La Croce family. Signora Ignazia, the mother, is a cheerfully sensual woman with four beautiful daughters, Mommina, Totina, Dorina, Nene, and a rather vague husband, Sampognetta. Signora Ignazia is a Neapolitan, who despises the provincialism of the Sicilians and is bringing up her daughters with a degree of freedom that is regarded as shameful by the neighbours. She particularly despises the young man who is courting her daughter Mommina, one Rico Verri, an air force officer. After Sampognetta is killed in a bar-room fight, Signora Ignazia and her daughters have to fend for themselves, which they do with some success. Totina becomes a famous singer, well able to keep her mother and sisters in luxury. Mommina, meanwhile, has opted out and married Verri. In a harrowing scene we see Mommina, with her two small daughters, imprisoned in their home by Verri, whose extreme jealousy has led him to this point of near-insanity. For Verri is not only jealous of the present, of the possibility of Mommina seeing or being seen by anyone else, he is jealous of the past, of the time before he even knew his wife, and he torments himself by imagining how many lovers she must have had.

The climax of the play is the scene where Mommina, having learned that her mother and sisters have come back to the village for a performance of *Il Trovatore*, tries to tell her children what theatre means. After the lengthy expositions of Hinkfuss earlier in the play, detailing all the devices that must be used and the conscious structuring that goes into the creation of a play, here we have the opposite point of view. Mommina tries to tell the children about the physical appearance of a theatre and a stage, then tries to explain the plot of the opera. Finally, overwhelmed by emotion, by the realization of how inadequate her description is and how bitterly frustrated her life has been, she tries to sing and falls dead on the floor. The stage directions reveal the terrible irony of such a death at such a moment:

> *The two children, more amazed than ever, don't even suspect a thing. They still think this is the theatre their mummy was explaining to them and they sit still on their little chairs, waiting.*

After this *coup de théâtre*, Mommina's relatives arrive too late, followed by Hinkfuss, unable to restrain his praise for the splendid scene he has just witnessed. The framing device of the Director and Actors setting up a play has run together with the play they have created, and in the final moments of *Tonight We Improvise* the Leading Lady who played Mommina comes slowly round after her death scene and Hinkfuss seizes the last word to apologize to the audience for all the confusion.

In the preface to *Six Characters* Pirandello expresses his contempt for the kind of theatre Hinkfuss tries to create, and the stage directions of *Tonight We Improvise* repeat that feeling. In Act II, Pirandello's stage directions tell us that Hinkfuss 'starts to beat about the bush' when he creates his elaborate Sicilian procession; this comic commentary on Hinkfuss' theatre practice increases during the Intermission scenes, at times becoming quite heavy-handed. As Edoardo Bruno has pointed out, Pirandello is taking up a very precise position against the spread of the grand spectacle theories of theatre, the type of theatre proposed by Max Reinhardt, for example, who has been suggested as a possible model for Hinkfuss.[4]

Although *Tonight We Improvise* was written in 1929, the views on theatre are similar to those expressed in his essay 'Spoken Action' (1899). Arguing for a quasi-metaphysical view of theatre, where characters come to life according to the commitment in their creation, Pirandello claims that the miracle of true theatre can only come to pass on one condition:

> that a language can be found which is itself spoken action, a living language that moves, the expression of immediacy, at one with action, the single phrase that must belong uniquely to a given character in a given situation: words, expressions, sentences that are not invented but are born when the author is fully at one with his creation so as to feel what it feels and want what it wants.

Pirandello is proposing a theatre of integrity, where no single element is given power over any other. It is a strikingly democratic ideal, but at the same time it is important to remember that Pirandello's plays were scripted down to the last detail, and his stage directions go far beyond the limits of merely suggesting ways of utilising space. In his biography of Pirandello, Giudice notes how Pirandello wrote *Tonight We Improvise* whilst in Berlin, where he went to the theatre as often as he could, and comments on the way in which Pirandello was 'both attracted and repelled by Reinhardt'. What Pirandello objected to was the way in which spectacle could become an end in itself, resulting in a diminution of the importance of the text, for there is no 'improvised' happening in Pirandello's theatre that is not carefully planned and scripted.

The ambiguity that Pirandello seems to have felt for spectacle theatre is apparent in *Tonight We Improvise*. Hinkfuss may be mocked and temporarily defeated by the actors, but he is also the figure who has some profound things to say about the nature of theatre. His elaborate stage effects are satirized, but the problem of their effectiveness remains, and the Sicilian procession, seen without the frame of Pirandello's derisory stage directions, can be an effective *coup de théâtre*. Moreover, although the Actors argue the case for a poor theatre, where stage effects and props take second place, the use of lighting in key moments such as Mommina's death scene is by no means a cheap trick but an important contribution to the final effect.

What seems to be happening in *Tonight We Improvise* is that Pirandello is debating with himself about the nature of theatre. Opposed in principle to spectacle theatre, he was also fascinated by it, and was sufficiently involved with practical theatre to understand the exigencies placed on a director. The satire against Hinkfuss is primarily directed against his attempts to control everything that happens, to use his position to exert power over the actors and to manipulate the audience. Hinkfuss attempts to shape into his own mould that which Pirandello argues is a fluid process.

The contrast between Hinkfuss' view of controlled theatre and spontaneous 'living' theatre is highlighted in the scene of Sampognetta's death. This character, played by the Old Comic Actor, is supposed to enter, fatally wounded, and die pathetically on the bosom of the nightclub Chanteuse, surrounded by his family. What happens is a comic anticlimax. The actors on stage break out of their roles and quarrel over the Leading Lady's improvization, forgetting to give Sampognetta his cue. He comes on stage furiously demanding an explanation. Hinkfuss' answer is to organize the scene as he planned it and get the actors to take up where they left off. They play

an exaggerated scene of grief and distress, until
Sampognetta, who has refused to speak during their
performance, announces that he cannot fulfil his role:

> I can't die, dear fellow, I just want to laugh when I see
> how good all these actors are and I can't die.

Hinkfuss argues, but Sampognetta remains intransigent. If
Hinkfuss wants him dead, he will just declare himself dead
and not waste any more time. He illustrates this by falling
'dead' onto the sofa – 'There's the scene for you! I'm
dead' – and refuses to co-operate because, he says, his
entrance was the most crucial part of the scene and that has
been ruined, leaving him with nothing important to do.
The absurdity of this scene contrasts strongly with the
subject matter. To the actor, the finality of death means
nothing, what matters is the effectiveness with which he
arouses emotions in his audience. Sampognetta describes
the scene that should have taken place:

> I was supposed to say all this in drunken delirium,
> running my bloody hands over my face – like this –
> covering myself with blood
> (*to the others*)
> am I covered in blood?
> (*and as they nod*)
> – good –
> (*continuing*)
> I was supposed to terrify you and make you cry.

After this speech he falls 'dead', the Leading Lady in her
role as Mommina bursts into tears and so affects the others
that they all start crying 'for real'. At this point Hinkfuss
interrupts, turns off the lights and ends the scene.

Sampognetta's stage death illustrates the fine line between pre-planned art and spontaneous gesture and feeling in theatre. He refuses to play the scene because his dramatic entrance has been ruined and mockingly summarizes what he should have done. Yet in spite of his mockery, his death is given reality by the distress of the others. What began as an angry take-off ends with the result the original scene hoped for: pathos.

After this scene, Hinkfuss tells the audience about stage deaths. The author, he claims, would have favoured an unobtrusive heart attack for the character, but Hinkfuss' spectacular theatre demands effect, with a highly melodramatic murder and death scene. Since the actor cannot actually die, what can be produced on stage is the visual impact of the moment of dying and this moment, Hinkfuss argues, should be presented as forcibly as possible. The shallowness of Hinkfuss' ideas is shown up in this address to the audience, for he explains the significance of Sampognetta's death with regard to the plot: since the family are now left to fend for themselves, Mommina marries Rico Verri in order to try and ease the burden. In short, Hinkfuss now talks about the death of Sampognetta as merely a link in the chain of events that make up the plot. What matters is not how he dies, merely that he does die in order to be got out of the way. This kind of lack of commitment is at the core of Pirandello's attack.

Tonight We Improvise is a huge, panoramic play about theatre making. It presents a wide range of angles to the problems of the amount of control that can and should be exerted over the processes of bringing theatre into being; on another level it presents the problem of the relativity of the freedom of mankind. 'Freedom and peace can only be had if one pays the price of ceasing to live', says Hinkfuss early in the play; in this case no-one ever can be free while still alive. Man is imprisoned in life, in the same way as the actor is confined to the stage in order to 'live'.

It is easy to see why, when discussing Beckett's *Waiting for Godot*, Raymond Williams talks about the characters being caught in a 'Pirandellian' situation where human beings are mutually destructive and frustrating.[5] The barren landscape used by Beckett, the prison settings used by Sartre, Pinter's closed rooms, Ionesco's device of using multiple sets to show that there is no way out may be compared to Pirandello's use of the actor trapped on stage in *Tonight We Improvise* as a metaphor for the spiritual and physical limitations of human existence.

The theatre trilogy is a set of plays that are structured explicitly around the processes of play-making, and in this sense they represent a unit that is distinctive from the rest of Pirandello's work. However, as any examination of Pirandello's total output reveals, his plays may all be described as metatheatre in that they are, in one way or another, plays about playing. From the three-act structures of many of the plays written in the early 1920s to the elaborate stage 'myths' of his later poetic drama, Priandello obsessively uses the form of the play to expound a vision of man's existential plight that is mirrored in the constraints of theatre. Like Shakespeare, Pirandello is concerned with using the stage as a metaphor for life, but unlike Shakespeare there is the added ironical dimension arising from Pirandello's particular vision of the dichotomy between art and life, between the fixed and the movable.

The plays of the theatre trilogy each develop one aspect of the processes of making a play: *Six Characters* focuses on the problem of the relationship between author, characterization in the written text and characterization in the performance text. *Each in His Own Way* focuses on the problem of the relationship between the play (in the playing the distinction between written and performance texts is blurred) and the audience, while *Tonight We Improvise* focuses on the problem of the creation of that performance text. What emerges strongly and clearly from all three plays is that Pirandello perceives theatre in dialectical terms, a series of dynamic relationships with no element being more or less significant than any other. Theatre is a process, it is the result of a set of separate and very different systems, each of equal importance. In his essay 'Theatre and Literature' (1918) Pirandello distinguishes between the idea of theatre that devalues the written text to the level of a *commedia dell' arte* scenario and one where the written text is treated seriously as part of the total process. In this essay he comes remarkably close to some of the views on theatre being formulated in the 20s and 30s in Russia and Czechoslovakia, among the groups later referred to as the Russian Formalists and Prague Structuralists. In his insistence on theatre as a dialectical set of relationships Pirandello might well be described as a theatre semiotician. In his study of the problems of theatre semiology, Patrice Pavis[6] argues that what still has to be explained is the interaction betweeen systems, the way in which the written text and performance text interact with each other and affect each other, and this is precisely what emerges from Pirandello's theatre trilogy. Opposed both to the view that holds the written text to be more important, in that performance must somehow realize it to the full, and also to the view that dismisses the written text as less essential, Pirandello's exposition of the complex debate in the theatre trilogy is of central importance to the development of a semiology of the theatre.

3
Playing with Truth/Life?

The problem with a chronological approach to Pirandello's writings is that his work does not divide easily into periods. True, the start of his theatre writing phase can be determined, just as the tendency for the earlier plays to revolve around problems of jealousy and adultery can be discerned, and the plays written towards the end of his life also have certain distinguishing characteristics. But because of Pirandello's insistence on the treatment of what may be called motifs in his work, the chronological approach is not the most helpful. Nor can his works be easily divided according to style and content material. The trilogy spans a nine year period with all kinds of other plays sandwiched in between. In good Pirandellian fashion, Pirandello's plays defy orderly categorization, and perhaps the best comparison to be made is that between Pirandello's oeuvre and an elaborate musical score, where leit-motifs recur and mingle throughout, at times clearly discernible and at other times submerged.

In the four plays discussed in this chapter, one such leit-motif recurs: the impossibility of determining absolute truth because of the layers of illusion with which man protects himself. At times Pirandello exposes the hollowness of such a belief in terms that are almost tragic, while elsewhere he stresses the comic absurdity of such a notion, and these two lines run parallel to each other, occasionally crossing in moments of high melodrama.

The four plays under consideration are *Right You Are, If You Think So* (first performed in Milan, in 1917, published in 1918); *The Rules of the Game* (first performed in Rome in 1918, published in 1919); *To Clothe the Naked* (first performed in Rome in 1922, published in 1923); *The Life I Gave You* (first performed in Rome in 1923, published in 1924). Although very different in many ways, these four plays typify the use of the favourite Pirandellian metaphor of life as a grotesque game being played for real by deluded mankind. Macbeth's famous soliloquy, in which life is compared to 'a poor player, who struts and frets his hour upon the stage and then is heard no more' echoes through these plays, as Pirandello uses the form of the play to expose the play-acting that lies at the heart of so-called true life.

'Right You Are (If You Think So)'

The basic construction of this play is in itself ironical, seeming at first to follow the pattern of the well-made thriller, where the audience is given a series of clues and watches the quest proceed through various fact-finding processes, each of which ends in failure. At the same time they are given a series of counter-clues by Laudisi, the cynical commentator figure, that point towards a different kind of discovery.

The stages in this thriller-plot are as follows: a group of Neighbours, all wealthy bourgeois members of small town society, are disturbed by the behaviour of a new arrival amongst them, one Signor Ponza who, they feel, is treating his mother-in-law, Signora Frola, with inhuman cruelty by not allowing her access to his wife. Details of Signora Frola's plight make the situation even more confused. The family having come from a village that was totally destroyed by an earthquake have lost their homes and all other relatives. This information makes the relationship between Signora Frola and Signor Ponza seem even more extraordinary. Questioned by the Neighbours, Signora Frola defends her son-in-law, claiming that the arrangement suits all three of them and denying any accusations of cruelty, but the Neighbours are still perplexed, determined to pursue the matter further in order to discover the 'truth'.

They seem to come closer to that truth when they talk to Signor Ponza, who tells them that his mother-in-law is mad, that his first wife, her daughter, is dead, and the woman he now lives with is his second wife who is no relation to the old lady at all. Keeping Signora Frola away from the house is a means of preserving her illusion that her daughter is still alive. But this explanation is then shattered by a further visit from Signora Frola, this time to claim that Signor Ponza is mad, and that she and her daughter agreed to the fiction of a second marriage after he had been convinced that his wife had died. By the end of the first act the Neighbours are further away from the truth than ever before, and now have two conflicting claims to contend with. The next two acts follow their attempts to prove the veracity of one or other of the versions, which turns out to be impossible since all documentary evidence and all other friends and relatives of the Ponza–Frola family have been destroyed in the earthquake. Finally, in an attempt to force the situation they confront Signor Ponza and Signora Frola with Signora Ponza, the daughter and/or wife, the missing link. Signora Ponza appears in the final scene of the play, heavily veiled, and when Signora Frola and Signor Ponza have gone, arm in arm, she tells the Neighbours the 'truth':

> SIGNORA PONZA: the truth? it's simply this: that I am indeed Signora Frola's daughter –
> EVERYONE (*sighs with satisfaction*) Ah.
> SIGNORA PONZA: (*immediately*) – and Signor Ponza's second wife –
> EVERYONE (*amazed, bewildered, intimidated*) – How can that be?
> SIGNORA PONZA: (*immediately*) – Yes. And for myself, I'm nobody. Nobody.
> THE PREFECT: Oh no madam, for yourself you must be one or the other.
> SIGNORA PONZA: No sir. For myself, I am whoever you believe me to be.

So the Neighbours' search, which has followed an entirely logical order through rational argument and a process of elimination, leads round in a complete circle. Not even the authority of the Prefect, the equivalent of the omniscient Inspector figure in the detective story, can be of any use. The play ends where it began, with a question mark, and the structure reinforces this. Act I opens with Laudisi's half-reflective 'So they've gone to the Prefect for help, have they?', pointing to the way the Neighbours try to define the problem in terms of their own bourgeois concepts of the world, in which the procedures of bureaucracy are seen to be reliable. Act III concludes with another question, Laudisi's ironical 'Are you satisfied now?', together with his bitter, mocking laughter.

Throughout the play Laudisi is concerned with the crisis of the individual driven by fear of formlessness to seek a definition behind which to hide. His attitude shifts from irritation to compassion and he makes several attempts to persuade the others to accept whatever illusion their beliefs may offer and not to proceed in their search for an absolute. He is on stage for most of the play, but is only highlighted at certain moments, remaining an observer for the rest of the time. Laudisi's presence is continually required by the Neighbours, even though he plays with them, for he has a dual function: his constant presence on stage reminds the audience of the irony of this quest for absolute truth, while to the Neighbours he represents the physical embodiment of their own doubts which must be overcome. His presence is sought because it is a challenge and, once fortified by the belief that truth must exist, the Neighbours are all prepared to try to fight him. It is easy to see why so many critics have seen Laudisi as 'Pirandello's own mouthpiece', a view reinforced by the fact that the figure of the compassionate ironist recurs so frequently in Pirandello's work.

Outside the search, and yet part of the action, Laudisi serves as a kind of commentator figure; his outbursts of laughter, five in all, occur at key moments in the play. All three acts end with Laudisi's laughter and the other two occasions are similarly break points in the action: he roars with laughter in Act I, sc. iii following a statement of conviction that the Prefect will be able 'to clear up this mystery and get at the truth', and again in Act II, sc. vi when Dina, the one character who seemed to have a chance of breaking out of the conventional pattern established by the others, shows that she is unable to act alone. On all five occasions his laughter is more a comment on what has happened than a mockery of any individual or individuals. His laughter is therefore more that of the compassionate humourist described in the essay 'On Humour' (1908), 'who has a sharper more subtle insight into life's realities' and who 'shows, or rather reveals in his fellow men profound differences between their appearance and the inner state of awareness'.

On three of the five occasions, Laudisi laughs at the word *verità* (truth), one of the keywords of the play. Pirandello's conscious use of keywords is a pattern clearly discernible in both his prose and theatre writings, and *Right You Are* is structured around three such words: *verità* and the verbs *vedere* (to see) and *credere* (to believe). Significantly, Laudisi uses *vedere* at the start of the play, and Signora Ponza uses *credere* at the end. *Vedere* is the first stage, the act of seeing, and, since sight is a sense impression, what man sees seems real to him. *Credere* is the second stage, the process by which what is seen is passed through the individual consciousness and an individual meaning is conferred on it. *Vedere* is one of the processes by which the external world registers on the internal; *credere* is a purely internal process, in no way restricted by anything outside the individual's consciousness. What Laudisi tries to do is to show the relativity of both stages; because man cannot know anything about another's process of *credere*, he cannot know that another's process of *vedere* is the same and can only assume that this must be the case. The Neighbours' search for truth derives from their refusal to acknowledge that others may see differently. They start from the assumption that, because they have seen Signor Ponza's family situation and attached a meaning to it, there can be no alternative perception. They look at the Ponza–Frola family as objects, denying that there might be any other way to interpret their situation. In this way the Ponza–Frola family become like actors, playing their parts to an audience, and Pirandello's stage directions reinforce this metaphor. The three strangers all wear black and are thus set apart in much the same way as the Six Characters are set apart by their physical appearance. When Signor Ponza and Signora Frola appear in the Agazzi household, they behave like actors performing to their public. The Neighbours watch them present their separate stories, then they watch the prearranged meeting between the two, and finally they watch the two encounter Signora Ponza. In every scene except the last, both claim that their daily life is an act, put on to preserve the illusion of the other.

In the last scene, all the threads are pulled together. The illusion that a name is an adequate definition is destroyed when Signora Ponza responds equally to being called both Lina and Giulia. In her brief speeches to the Neighbours Signora Ponza uses all three key words, beginning with *vedere*, in the line 'There has been a tragedy here, as you can see. . . .' So much is clear – the three strangers are in mourning, Signor Ponza and Signora Frola show signs of distress on several occasions and their arrival in the village is framed by the disastrous earthquake. What the Neighbours can see, therefore, is sufficient to arouse compassion, the outward appearances alone testify to suffering.

Next Signora Ponza deals with *verità*, insisting that she exists equally for both parties and that both existences are equally valid. This, she claims, is the truth. She has accepted that the self cannot see itself and can only know itself through its reflection via the perceptions of another.

Signora Ponza's truth is that she is whoever she is believed to be, and the last word she utters is *crede* (believe). She is the physical embodiment of a concept that the reality of each individual is arbitrary; this discovery, that a general reality does not exist, creates terror for the Neighbours. For through such a discovery comes a recognition of the need to exist through others, of the impossibility of imposing man-made boundaries in an infinite universe. At the same time, Signora Frola and Signor Ponza leave the stage united as never before in the play, precisely because that infinity which has destroyed the cosy world of the Neighbours makes each of their beliefs equally valid.

The defeat of the Neighbours' search illustrates the fallacy of man's attempt to impose his own order on a limitless universe. But in spite of this there is still a means of escape, through illusion. Laudisi's advice to the Neighbours to use their imaginations finally becomes the advice of the play as a whole and nothing will disturb an illusion of serenity but the faint sound of ironical laughter.

Right You Are has been frequently performed, both in Italian and in English, and remains one of the most popular of Pirandello's plays, but its reputation has suffered somewhat from being compared disparagingly to the 'experimental' plays. Robert Brustein, for example, describes the play as 'a fairly conventional exercise in the mode of the grotesque', while Eric Bentley describes it as the most famous statement of Pirandello's relativism. More recently, Olga Ragusa has perceptively noted that the play is at the same time 'popular and difficult', and sees it as far more than an exercize piece in a theatre of ideas.

The use of keywords and tight structuring of the play, full of moments of comic anticlimax and scenes where the Ponza–Frola family 'perform' for the Neighbours, reflect Pirandello's continued use of the stage–life dichotomy as a metaphor for the illusion–reality dichotomy of his philosophy. *Right You Are* can thus be also seen as a play that is self-consciously about itself, where the deliberate structuring of the scenes is not meant to create an illusion of verisimilitude but is meant to deliberately draw attention to the artifices of the processes of theatre.

'The Rules of the Game'

The Italian title, *Il giuoco delle parti*, means literally 'the game of roles', whereas the accepted English title alters the emphasis from role-playing to the notion of rules that might apply in the game, an idea that shifts the meaning of the play in a slightly different direction. The game of role-playing which Pirandello sees as an intrinsic part of man's life, since it is the only way in which he can delude himself that his existence is justified, is another favourite leit-motif in his work. Pirandello suggests that, to protect himself against the devastating vision of constant motion, man plays a series of games, some voluntary and some involuntary. The image of the mask, the false face that may conceal other faces, is basic to Pirandello's theatre, as is the mirror that can strip away a mask by reflecting a distorting image. In *The Rules of the Game*, role-playing on both levels can be seen in operation. The irony comes when the two levels meet and clash, and Leone destroys the game Silia and Guido have built up in order to trap him.

The plot of this play is more straightforward than many. Leone Gala, a figure reminiscent of Laudisi, appears to condone the affair his wife Silia is having with Guido. Leone and Silia are separated, although Leone visits his wife every evening for half an hour, one of the conditions of the separation. In the first act Guido endeavours to understand the relationship between Leone and Silia, puzzled by their arrangement and utterly bewildered when Silia insists that Leone will not allow her to be free. Chance then offers Silia the way to get back at him. Trying to hit the departing Leone with an egg-shell she accidentally hits someone else, one of four young men looking for a prostitute named Pepita. Silia realizes that in their drunken state they mistook her for Pepita when they burst into her apartment, believing that the egg-shell gesture was an invitation to come up and see her. She plays along with them just long enough to discover the name of one of them and then, when her maid and other neighbours come to her assistance, she claims they have assaulted her and must publicly answer for it.

In Act II Silia engineers a duel between Leone and Miglioriti, the young man whose identity she discovered. When Leone agrees, in spite of her realization that he understands that she is hoping he will die, the relationship between husband and wife moves towards a point almost of tenderness as each confesses to feeling intense pain. Silia claims to find solace only in sleep and dreams, whilst Leone declares that he copes with his existential anguish by setting himself apart from human emotions. Then in Act III, as the climax approaches, the mood changes yet again. Leone refuses to fight and Guido, his second, is compelled to take his place in order to save face. Silia arrives and realizes what Leone has done, how he has turned the game to his own advantage and made Guido fall into his own trap. In a moment of unique self-revelation in the play, Leone drops the mask of indifference to declare to Silia that he has punished both her and her lover in this way. The play ends with Guido mortally wounded off stage. As Silia runs out screaming, Leone stands motionless, barely responding to his valet's announcement that breakfast is ready. The mask that protected him has been torn away and there is no way out, not even through illusion.

The basic game of the play is defined by Leone in Act I when talking to Guido:

> LEONE: It's a sad thing, you know, when you can see through the game.
>
> GUIDO: What game?
>
> LEONE: Oh . . . this one here if you like. The whole game. The game of life.

The only way to be safe in this game, Leone claims, is to know how to defend oneself, and throughout the play we see him in a defensive position, carefully avoiding the pitfalls that are laid in his way. His compensation, as he explains to Guido, lies in the playing of his own type of game, 'the game of the intellect that clarifies all muddiness of feelings and fixes in placid, precise lines everything that moves so tumultuously within you'. But in the last resort Leone's game fails him. Not even the power of his calm, logical approach to life can save him from the pain he feels when he faces up to his love-hatred for Silia.

The relationship between Leone and Silia recalls an R. D. Laing case history. It is apparent from the beginning that Silia has little in common with her lover Guido. In the opening scene Silia tries to describe her sense of dissatisfaction with life, her 'desire for the impossible', as she puts it, while Guido responds with uncomprehending platitudes. When she tells him how Leone suffocates her through the power he still exerts over her, Guido cannot understand at all. Later in the play, in his conversation with Leone, he also fails to understand what is being said to him. He is equally distant from both husband and wife.

The scenes between Silia and Guido and between Leone

and Guido that take place in Act I show two sides of the same problem. Silia articulates her feelings of unhappiness, Leone claims that he has learned the art of mastering his emotions and plays the part of the cynical master. What emerges from both these scenes is the depth and intensity of both Silia and Leone compared to the shallowness of Guido. Husband and wife are set up for the audience as ideal partners for each other, and in the conventions of the love-story of misunderstanding the climax of the play would be their reconciliation. Pirandello, however, does no such thing. The relationship between Silia and Leone, which at times moves into profound tenderness, can be understood as yet another metaphor for life. Locked together, they look for a means of escape but cannot find one. Silia's mistake is to assume that Leone's death would provide a solution, but once she has embarked on this dangerous game she becomes uneasy. The contrast between her uneasiness and Leone's calm good humour provides much of the irony of the central part of the play.

In Act II all the ingredients for a farce are provided: the audience knows what Guido and Silia are trying to do, but at the same time they can see that Leone is playing cat and mouse with the guilty pair. 'You have to play your part as I have to play mine. That's what the game's about', Leone tells Guido in Act II, sc. iii and later, in sc. vi he tells Silia that he is completely protected by the air of indifference that he assumes no matter what:

> I live in such a climate, my dear, that I can afford to care about nothing – caring as little about life as I do about death. So imagine how I feel about being laughed at by people with their petty ideas and opinions. Don't be afraid. I've understood this game.

Leone's final sentence is, of course, highly ambiguous and works on several levels. The audience know that he is referring to earlier conversations in the play where he had expressed similar views on the nature of the life-game, but it becomes ironical in that he is both victim of a game designed to lead to his death and player of yet another game that will ultimately lead to Guido's death in his place. When he plays his hand and refuses to fight, his language is full of game references:

> Get away with you, yesterday when you were here with my wife you looked as if you were on a seesaw, going up and down, with me in the middle, getting my balance and then steadying you two. Oh, you thought you were playing games with me, with my life, didn't you? Well, you missed your target friends. I've played you out!

The title of the play derives from Leone's speech immediately prior to this moment of seeming triumph, when he defends his decision not to fight, claiming that Guido must take his place according to 'the game of roles'. This reversal of events is entirely logical: since Silia and Guido have involved him in a duel because of his role as husband, he now hands over that role to Guido who usurped it from him in all but name by becoming Silia's lover:

> I issued the challenge as the husband because he couldn't do it for my wife. But as for fighting, no. As for fighting, well . . . (*to Guido*) you know the reason don't you? it's nothing to do with me. So there you are, I'm not fighting, you are!

It is significant that Pirandello chose to make this the

play that the Actors are supposed to be rehearsing at the start of *Six Characters*. The scene that the Director begins to read out to the Actors is the opening of Act II, where Leone, dressed in a cook's hat and apron, is beating an egg in a bowl, together with his butler, Filippo, dressed identically and also beating an egg. The Actors in *Six Characters* complain about the ridiculousness of this scene and the Director tries to offer a quick interpretation: the egg sequence is important, he says, because the egg is symbolic. The shell signifies the empty form of reason, the yolk is the blind force of instinct. Leone is reason, Silia is instinct and the game of role-playing turns the characters into cardboard cut-outs of themselves. The Actors still don't understand, the Director admits that he doesn't either and at this point the Six Characters appear and interrupt.

In this opening scene of *Six Characters* Pirandello is satirizing both the idea of a Director who cannot understand his chosen text and the stupidity of facile interpretations based on the significance of symbols. 'I didn't win, but I didn't lose either', he wrote to his son Stefano after the first night of *The Rules of the Game* in 1918, for although Ruggero Ruggeri's performance as Leone Gala was praised, the play was widely misunderstood. So the Actors in *Six Characters* complain about the device of the egg in much the same way as critics have stressed the symbolic significance of the egg which recurs at different times in *The Rules of the Game*. Silia's plot is set in motion by her misthrowing of the egg-shell, which she happens to have with her after trying to use it to mock Leone, who first introduces the question of eggs in his talk with Guido in Act I. Telling Guido that the way to deal with life is to abstract feelings from logic, he suddenly asks Guido to imagine an egg. When Guido asks why,

Leone gives him a succinct answer: 'Just to give you a new image of cases and concepts!' Leone then goes on to suggest that if an egg were to fall out of the sky one day, anyone not prepared for it would probably let it smash to the ground, whereas anyone really ready would be able to catch it, suck out the yolk and use the empty shell as a plaything until ready to crush it and throw it away. The egg is therefore not so much a symbol as an example used by Leone to both illustrate and defend the particular way he has chosen to play out his own game. Ironically, just as Leone's cleverness finally causes him to lose, so the egg takes on a life of its own, precipitating events and acting as a catalyst.

What emerges strongly is the way in which the games intensify and develop. Leone's example of the egg is turned into a physical object and used in various ways, and the play itself is part of a game being played between Pirandello and the audience. On the face of it, this is a three-act, naturalistic play with clearly defined characters and a tight plot structure, but at the same time it is full of question marks, and the balance between farce and despair is very finely drawn. No-one wins anything in spite of all the games and Leone's carefully wrought system of defence is seen to be as hopeless as Silia's sense of frustrated longing. As with *Right You Are*, the play is unfolded for the audience in layer after layer, like the skin of an onion, only to reveal that there is no central core after all, no final solution and, in Leone's case, nothing to be said or done. The parallels between the end of this play and the end of *Waiting for Godot* are startlingly close, and the bleakness of such a moment is intensified by the dark comedy of what has gone on before.

Luigi Pirandello

'To Clothe the Naked'

In *The Rules of the Game* there is a strong part for a
woman. As Pirandello began to write increasingly for
Marta Abba, female protagonists came to be an important
feature in his theatre. One of his most memorable figures is
Ersilia Drei, the protagonist of *To Clothe the Naked*, a
pathetic but tough character, struggling for survival in a
world that has no pity for her. Although this play is
dedicated to Marta Abba, the leading role was originally
played not by her but by Maria Melato, a well-known
actress who had appeared in a number of Pirandello's
plays, including *Right You Are (If You Think So)*. The
range of possibilities offered by the role of Ersilia Drei has
meant that this play has been revived more frequently than
many of Pirandello's other works. A notable British
production was the 1963 revival at the Royal Court, with
Diane Cilento in the leading role, in her own translation of
the play.

To Clothe the Naked is constructed around a moral
dilemma and once again takes up the question of the
impossibility of determining a single truthful version of a
story. As with *Each in His Own Way* the details of Ersilia's
life emerge gradually, through a series of discussions
between other characters. This building-block technique,
where each newly discovered fact adds an additional layer
of significance, is one of Pirandello's favourite methods.
Another feature which this play shares with much of
Pirandello's work is the ever-present idea of death and
catastrophe that lurks behind even the funniest moments.
The bourgeois room depicted on the stage conceals the
horrors of suicide, prostitution and brutal accidental death
that are part of the world outside its boundaries.

The protagonist, Ersilia Drei, is a young woman who

1. Luigi Pirandello in his study in Rome in 1913.

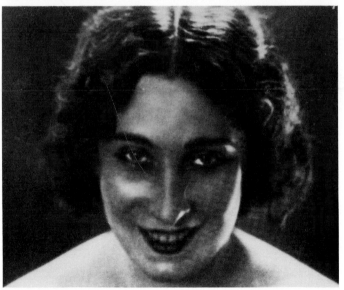

2. Marta Abba.

3. *Six Characters in Search of an Author*, 1923.

4. *Six Characters in Search of an Author*, 1923.

5. Pirandello, Pitoëff and Benjamin Crémieux at the dress rehearsal of *Six Characters* in 1923.

THE NEW PIRANDELLO PLAY.

A scene from the play (as yet without title) which will be produced at the Huddersfield Theatre Royal to-night. Diego Spina is restrained from killing his wife's lover. Left to right: Cico (Mr. C. Lefeaux), Diego Spina (Mr. Donald Wolfit), Lawyer (Mr. E. Millington), Lucio (Mr. A. van Gyseghem), Sara (Miss Edith Sharpe), Dr. Gionni (Mr. Alan Wheatley).

6. *Lazarus*. The first production was staged in Huddersfield in 1929.

7. *Tonight We Improvise* staged by the Piccolo Teatro of Milan, in Paris in 1949.

8. *The Mountain Giants* directed by Giorgio Strehler at the Piccolo Teatro of Milan in 1966.

9. *The Mountain Giants*, Milan, 1966.

10. *Henry IV*. Rex Harrison in the title role. Her Majesty's Theatre, London, 1974.

has attempted suicide shortly before the action of the play begins. She is befriended by Lodovico Nota, an aging writer, whose interest in her has been aroused by a newspaper report of the facts leading up to her decision to end her life. In the first act we see him using her as living material, building up a scenario into which he can comfortably fit her, a process that she seems only too happy to comply with initially. Ersilia's story, as such, is deeply unhappy. She had been dismissed from her job as nanny at the home of the Italian consul in Smirne, after the accidental death of the Consul's baby daughter. She had also been involved with a naval officer, Franco Laspiga, who left her to become engaged to another woman from his own class. Finding herself alone and abandoned on all sides, Ersilia turned briefly to prostitution and then tried to kill herself. Throughout the first act Lodovico pushes her ever further to tell him more about the circumstances that drove her to despair, especially after the arrival of a newspaper reporter who is being threatened with a libel action by the Consul on account of the story he has written about Ersilia. Details of the child's death and the relationship between the Consul and his wife given to the paper by Ersilia are being questioned and the reporter has come to see whether she is willing to change her story and help him out. Already by the end of the first act the idea of multi-faceted truth that changes and shifts around, offering no protection anywhere, is established as a dominant motif.

Ersilia's distress at the reporter's questioning of her version increases when Franco Laspiga, her former boy friend, comes to make amends for what he has done. Convinced that she tried to kill herself for love of him, he now tells her he has jilted his fiancée and offers to marry her. Forced into another corner by this news, Ersilia at first tries to put him off by arousing his disgust, and tells him about her prostitution, but he insists on claiming responsibility for her plight. Finally, dropping all pretence she resorts to plain speaking:

> I tell you I was pretending; I tell you it isn't true; I tell you I lied. And I'll repeat that. It wasn't your fault. It was just life. This life that's still going on – Oh God – how awful it is – and that I've never been able to get into any coherent sort of shape. What else do I have to say to you to get rid of you?

At this point of frank honesty she is precipitated against yet another barrier: the arrival of Consul Grotti himself. The scene between Ersilia and the Consul, as each accuses the other of being responsible for the child's death, is the most powerful point in the play except for the final scene. What emerges from this scene is a new twist; the two had been lovers and the child had fallen to her death from a balcony while they were together. The Consul starts by attacking Ersilia, brutally accusing her of being a whore and a liar, but ends by acknowledging his own passionate need for her which is more than she can bear. Hounded on all sides by the two men she once loved, who are unable to listen to her and insist on imposing their own version of events in spite of what she says, and hounded also by society in general, personified by Signora Onoria, the uncouth, bourgeois landlady, Ersilia takes poison again and succeeds. In her final speech which ends the play she explains why she had embroidered the facts of her life, leaving out certain details and elaborating others: all she wanted, she claims, was a garment with which to dress up decently at the point of death, since that garment had been denied her in life. The myth of being a loved and abandoned fiancée was just such a garment and she had used it, as she puts it, to cover the nakedness of her existence. Now, with all the details of her past affairs made public, she sees all hope of covering gone:

> Go away now. Let me die in silence, naked. Go away. Surely now I can say that I don't want to see anyone or listen to anyone? Go away, and you, go and tell your wife, you, go and tell your fiancée that this dead woman – yes, look at me – couldn't even clothe herself.

Although Ersilia dies naked, bereft of all the illusions of love with which she had tried to mask the sordidness of her love life, for the audience she dies with immense dignity. She alone, of all the characters in the play, has any kind of integrity and the struggles she undergoes through the course of the play win audience sympathy over to her completely. For Ersilia is a victim of the vicissitudes of life, as she herself sees, but she is also the victim of two shallow, power-seeking men who have used her for their own selfish purposes and, in a sense, the victim of Lodovico Nota and the press who use her life as copy for their readers. Ersilia may have had small middle-class ambitions – to be a fiancée, then a decent wife, and so define herself in terms of the strictest family morality – but she is cheated of this dream by the corruption of men in positions of power and authority.

The keywords in the play point to the contrast between Ersilia's vision of happiness and the social forces that combine to deprive her of it. There are, as might be expected, continual references to nakedness and clothing, since this is the predominant metaphor of the play, and the other two keywords are *strada* (street) and *riparare* (to make amends, to repay). This is the verb used repeatedly by both men. When Franco Laspiga arrives he insists that he has come 'to make amends, sir, to make amends. To throw myself at her feet, to ask for forgiveness', while the Consul tries to force Ersilia to make love with him so that they can both make amends for their guilt over the dead child and share their unhappiness. In Act III Laspiga and the Consul sympathize with one another over Ersilia's stubborn refusal to accept the sacrifice each feels he is making by offering to make amends. What emerges from Ersilia's rejection of them both is the self-centredness of their supposed generosity. Neither of them loves her as she wants to be loved, but both are driven to her by a combination of lust and unwillingness to be perceived as dishonourable in the eyes of society at large; both have only responded to her desperation because of the story in the newspapers, not because they cared in any way for her. This is the final indignity that Ersilia cannot contemplate.

References to the street run through the play as a reminder of the lack of security and protection in life. Lodovico's room, with its wealth of comfortable furnishings, is constantly invaded by the sounds of the street outside. Early in Act I those street sounds change to screams of agony and shouting as an old man is crushed to death by a car just under the window. This incident is witnessed by Ersilia, Lodovico and Signora Onoria, who comment on it with horror. Its symbolic significance is very clear. The street, like Brecht's city jungle, is the world of unforeseen violence and terror where sudden painful death can strike one down and yet barely disturb the lives of others who may witness it by chance. Ersilia, whose sensitivity is greater than that of any of the other characters, is the one person who has understood what the street signifies. As she tells the Consul in Act III, her decision to die came from understanding how helpless she was without the support, albeit illusory, of social structures and conventions. The main convention that Ersilia has been deprived of is bourgeois respectability, the honour and status that would have been conferred on her by being a married woman. The last words she speaks, to the Consul and to Franco Laspiga, draw the contrast between their women, the wife and the fiancée, and herself. But the play also satirizes that idea of respectability, showing up the hollowness behind a life-system based on canons of social behaviour rather than on the needs of individuals, and the satire is focused upon the figure of Signora Onoria, the landlady. Onoria is a weathervane, whose views change according to circumstances. When she first appears, in the opening scene of the play, she attacks Ersilia for being no better than she should be and accuses Lodovico of immoral behaviour by bringing Ersilia to stay in his rooms. She is only silenced when Lodovico threatens to leave, showing how her standards of decency are subordinate to her mercenary interests. By the start of Act II, however, once she has learned that Ersilia is a kind of celebrity, Onoria's attitude changes completely and she defends Ersilia, using the image of the creature attacked by savage animals, a motif that Ersilia returns to in her final speech:

> She makes me think about how you sometimes see a poor lost little creature surrounded by savage dogs in the street, and – there's no explaining why this happens – the gentler it is, the more the others attack it and bite it and tear it apart.

But by Act III Onoria has changed her mind again, following the visits of the various men to the house and the gossip of Emma, the maidservant. Now she turns on

Ersilia once again, accusing Lodovico of stupidity in lending her money and offering to help. The status of the Consul and Franco Laspiga has convinced her that Ersilia is the evil woman she first took her for, and Laspiga's haste to recount the story of Ersilia's responsibility for the child's death confirms her in this view.

Onoria judges by appearances in Act I, and is prompted to kindness in Act II by brief contact with Ersilia, the rather plaintive and appealing human being. By Act III she is again judging by appearances and hearsay, convinced by the facts she has heard from the Consul and Laspiga. At this point in the play Lodovico steps out of his role as author, searching for material for his writing, and makes one of the most profound statements in the play about the relativity of truth:

> Facts! Facts! Facts, dear sir, are what one takes them to be, so in spirit they are facts no longer, just life that appears to be one way or another. Facts are the past, when the soul gives in . . . and life abandons them. So I don't believe in facts.

Lodovico has learned that life cannot be reduced to schema and that facts will vary according to who attempts to catalogue them. Ersilia's version of what has happened to her is not the same as anyone else's, it is far more complex than anything Lodovico could produce. And already, in the relationship between Ersilia and Lodovico we can see a recurrence of the theme that dominates plays such as *Diana and Tuda* or, in a slightly different way, *Tonight We Improvise*, that of the distance between what is imagined and what is lived. When Ersilia tells Lodovico that she would like to be as he imagines her, he replies that she is much more attractive as herself. Ersilia is in search of an author to throw a garment of beauty and respectability over her story, while Lodovico is in search of living passion to fix in the works he creates. Both, in their own way, are doomed to failure.

Ersilia's tragedy, on the surface, is her failure to achieve respectability, but on a deeper level her tragedy is the lack of any creative outlet, and the coexistence of these levels gives the play a particular ambiguity. The Fascist ideology of women exalted the natural creativity of motherhood. Women were the pillars of society, the fixed points of reference for men engaged in struggle against enemy hordes, and marriage took on an almost mystical significance. It has often been noted that Mussolini set great store by his image as Bridegroom to Italia, the motherland. When he appealed to Italian women to hand in their gold wedding rings to help the war effort, millions rushed to exchange their rings for the metal symbol of honour that showed they were wedded to Il Duce and his new utopia. Yet in spite of this, and in spite of his commitment to Mussolini at this time, Pirandello's plays show up the shallowness of so-called respectability. *To Clothe the Naked* is a particularly scathing attack on the double standard that judged some women as worthy to be wives and condemned others to a life of exclusion. It is indeed ironic that Onoria, the property-owning married woman, has everything that Ersilia most desires and is at the same time one of the most unsympathetic characters in the play. Pirandello's own position vis-à-vis marriage is not clear-cut. Significantly he noted that Mussolini disliked this play, although he had praised other works such as *Six Characters* and *Henry IV*. Moreover, although in many of his plays Pirandello allows the audience to form its own views and debate with the characters as the action progresses, sympathy is weighted in favour of

Ersilia, the outcast. It is not so unexpected, then, that it did not find favour with Mussolini.

'The Life I Gave You'

The Life I Gave You was also written for a specific actress, but one of a very different kind. Eleonora Duse, probably the greatest Italian actress of her time, was getting on in years – 'silver-haired', according to Silvio d'Amico, who recounted the story of her involvement with *The Life I Gave You* – and wanted to appear in a play by the new fashionable dramatist. Pirandello wrote the play for her but Duse never appeared in it. She seems to have made excuses of illness, but Silvio d'Amico tells how scandalized she was by what appeared to her to be distasteful plot material, and Pirandello's son Stefano adds that Duse objected to the play on religious grounds. Whatever the reasons, she decided not to do it, and the leading role was performed by Alda Borelli. After its first run the play was not revived for twenty years.

Although Duse never appeared in the play, it is possible to see ways in which Pirandello structured it for her style of acting. The protagonist, Donn'Anna, has all the crucial speeches and is on stage longer than anyone else. She is also the centre of a number of scenes that appear almost as *tableaux vivants*, such as the moment of her first appearance, coming out of the room in which her dead son is lying, or the final scene where she at last breaks down and lets out her grief in desperate weeping. The play is full of stage pictures, of carefully designed points in which an actress as used to dominating stage space as Duse was, can hold the attention of the audience. And as if to increase Donn'Anna's statue even further, there are also moments of powerful visual impact where no characters are present on stage. The opening scene, with peasant women praying outside the dead man's room, is one such moment; this scene is held for several minutes of strong tension until the entrance of Fiorina and Don Giorgio, the priest. Another such moment comes in Act II, just before the arrival of Lucia, when the stage remains empty for a time, while a piece of furniture moves slightly and a curtain twitches. The stage directions explain these curious movements:

> *Who knows what kind of things happen, unseen by anyone, in the shadows of empty rooms where someone is lying dead?*

The play begins with a death; Donn'Anna's only son has just died, and her sister, Fiorina, discusses the tragedy with the parish priest. They try to comfort Donn'Anna, who appears unable to accept the idea of her son's death, and keeps insisting that he is still alive for her and within her:

> It's enough for memory to be alive, that's what I say, because dreams are life, after all. My son as I see him: alive. – Not the one that's in there. Try to understand me.

The dead man had been in love with a married woman, and Donn'Anna finds a letter that he had started to write, urging her to leave her family and come to him. Donn'Anna decides to finish the letter and send it, since she sees this as a way of prolonging her son's life – the life in her mind – through the woman he loved.

When Lucia arrives in response to the letter, Donn'Anna prevaricates, unable to tell her what has happened. Believing that she has been abandoned by her lover, Lucia breaks down and tells Donn'Anna that she is pregnant. Donn'Anna responds with wild joy:

> Oh my daughter, my daughter! Is he truly alive in you?
> Did he go away and still leave a life – his life – in you?

But in sending the letter to Lucia, Donn'Anna has had to compromize and has also written to Francesca, Lucia's mother. In Act III Francesca meets Donn'Anna, who tries to explain why she has still not told Lucia the truth. Francesca is appalled, but before either mother can talk to her, Lucia rushes in and realizes almost instinctively what has happened. The extent of Lucia's grief destroys any illusion that he might still be 'alive' in her mind in the way Donn'Anna has hoped.

Although so much of the play focuses on Donn'Anna, there is an important secondary line that runs together with the main plot – the problematic relationship between Fiorina and her children, Lida and Flavio. In Act I, Donn'Anna talks to her sister about the sense of loss she had felt when she discovered that in his absence from her, her son had become a man she did not know:

> You think my son has just died, don't you? He didn't just die now for me. I cried all my tears in secret, which is why I haven't any left to cry now when I saw him come home as another person, who wasn't anything like my son at all. . . .
> Life can treat a mother so cruelly: it takes a son away from her and changes him. He was someone else and I didn't know it. Dead, and I kept him alive in me.

Later, in Act II, we see how Fiorina's children repeat the same pattern and how she realizes that she does not know them any longer. Fiorina's growing awareness of the changes that have taken place in her children makes Donn'Anna's pain all the more comprehensible.

When Lucia understands what Donn'Anna has tried to do, she insists on staying with her. For an instant, Donn'Anna seizes upon this as a solution – Lucia's baby will be her own son reborn, she will have him back again through his own child. Then when Francesca intervenes, insisting that Lucia must go back to her husband and other children, back into the world, Donn'Anna gives way, realizing that the baby never will be her son, he will be Lucia's. Her role as mother is over forever, and she is at last able to weep. Lucia still says she will stay, but Donn'Anna has finally seen the extent of her loss. Death is not so much the cessation of bodily functions, it is the awareness of loss. Fiorina's children are lost to her, just as Donn'Anna's son is lost. 'This is death', Donn'Anna says in her final speech, it is the helplessness of being alive and subject to inevitable change and decay. The despair of the mother in this final scene is not offset by moments of farcical humour as in most of Pirandello's plays. Together with *Henry IV* and *Diana and Tuda* he designated *The Life I Gave You* as a tragedy.

The keywords of the play are obvious from the start: *vita* (life) and *morte* (death) are used in ironic juxtaposition. At the end of Act II, Donn'Anna is alone on stage, in another striking stage picture, after Lucia has gone to bed. She utters just one word: *Vive* (He's alive). But by the end of the play, when she has had to come to terms with the many layers of death, her mood is very different:

What shall I do here? – This is really death, daughter. Things have to be done, whether we want to or not –

and things have to be said. – Right now we have to look up a timetable, then get a carriage to the station – travel. We are the poor busy dead ourselves. Tormenting ourselves – consoling ourselves – calming ourselves. This really is death!

Earlier, trying to convince Francesca that what she has done is the right thing, Donn'Anna explains that her son is still alive both in her heart and in Lucia's. Francesca brutally reminds her that her son is a corpse, and Donn'Anna tries to tell her she is wrong: death for Lucia, she argues, is the life she must lead with a man she does not love, whereas life is the feeling she has for the man she does love, regardless of whether his physical body is present. But Donn'Anna's illusion is doomed to failure. She may have been able to create an illusion for herself, but it cannot be shared and when she tries, even her own is shattered.

This is a play primarily about mothers, who give life but are unable to control it and suffer as they see their children slip away from them. The image of the suffering Mother in *Six Characters* is developed in this play and fleshed out, through the figures of Donn'Anna, Fiorina and Francesca, with a second generation mother, Lucia. In Act II Donn'Anna tells Fiorina that the fact of being a mother gives her courage – having borne a child and fed him and feared nothing, now she 'eats life for him'. But Fiorina is just beginning to understand what Donn'Anna told her previously, that her children, the ones she knows, are dying before her eyes as she loses contact with them and this is the greatest fear of all.

Pirandello's description of life as a continuous moving river that cannot be stopped is given an additional dimension in this play. Donn'Anna's attempt to beat death is a particularly poignant example of the helplessness of human beings who are swept along in the flood tide of that life-river. The play ends on a very dark note, with resignation to suffering as the inevitable end. Donn'Anna has lost her will to try and fight back against the forces that have robbed her of her child.

The idea of the suffering mother whose power is great enough for her to try to challenge even the forces of death is one which emerges later in Pirandello's work in a more positive form. In *The New Colony*, for example, it is a mother and child who alone are saved after the destruction of the world. It is as if Pirandello moved from writing about the depths of human unhappiness to creating plays about an alternative system in which certain positive forces might survive, and in so doing tried to create a new type of theatre. Those positive forces are represented by women.

At the time of writing the four plays discussed in this chapter, Pirandello was still some way away from writing his 'myths', as he later termed them. The main concern in these plays is not the positing of any alternative system, but the exposure of the contradictions inherent in the existing one. From these plays emerges a vision of a society on the edge of collapse, where bourgeois values have eaten away at the mainstay of life, human compassion. In all four plays people play games in order to cope, and although Donn'Anna's pathetic game is an attempt to beat death, it is as illusory as the search for absolute truth that the Neighbours pursue in *Right You Are*. All the plays, whether farcical or tragic, are built around ugliness and unhappiness. In *Right You Are*, the Ponza–Frola family have been driven from their homes by an earthquake, in *The Rules of the Game* the characters are caught up in a duel that leads to one man's death, in *To Clothe the Naked*

Ersilia has tried prostitution and suicide as a way of punishing herself for her part in a child's death, and in *The Life I Gave You* Donn'Anna's only son lies dead as the play begins. These dark events are paralleled by details of the disintegrating social fabric in which the characters find themselves: in *The Rules of the Game* and *To Clothe the Naked*, the respectable mask of marriage conceals adultery and deceit, while the comedy of *Right You Are* and the tragedy of *The Life I Gave You* have in common the destruction of a family. Moreover, in all four plays the tension between classes is very evident. The world of these plays is a world where lawyers, prefects, doctors and consuls have exalted views of their own importance and use their positions of power to manipulate others. In *The Life I Gave You* Fiorina's children come back to her as sophisticated city dwellers, full of stories of parties and expensive consumer goods, members of a world which Fiorina cannot enter and which is depicted as shallow and frivolous. On stressing the links between Pirandello's world vision and that of later Existentialist thinkers, it is often forgotten that the bourgeois world his characters inhabit is exactly contemporary with that of Scott Fitzgerald and both writers share a concern for depicting the hollowness of the new post-war order.

The crisis of moral values that Pirandello depicts again and again in his plays (and he wrote nine other plays in the period spanned by the four discussed in this chapter) is, nevertheless, treated with ambiguity. Even though he may attack the shallow posing of authority figures and show up the unhappiness of individuals caught in the traps set by society at large, his attacks are not made with any reforming zeal, but rather with the ironic detachment of one of the characters of his own creation, a Laudisi figure, or a Lodovico Nota. As Diego Fabbri has pointed out, in

an article entitled 'Pirandello poeta drammatico'
('Pirandello, dramatic poet'):

> he is not a *reformer*. What is *tragic* in him comes
> precisely from this: he does not have any model to
> propose or suggest, let alone impose on anyone. On the
> other hand, what would such a model serve? He is like a
> policeman who has to be satisfied with shadowing and
> following and inquiring round after his subjects without
> ever being able to stop them and make an arrest and
> handcuff them in the name of some law or other.[1]

In these four plays Pirandello makes no arrests at all, he
merely points an accusing finger and exposes the
inadequacy of the games his characters play with life.

4
The Mask of Identity

Throughout his writing career Pirandello remained fascinated by the ironies inherent in belief in a single absolute identity. Many of his plays and prose writings centre on the clash between a fixed notion of identity and the multi-faceted nature of man's social role. The problem of the shapelessness of identity offered both tragic and comic possibilities, and Pirandello explored the range of ironic contrasts in the dichotomy between the mask, which may be assumed as a disguise, and the face that may or may not exist behind it. This particular preoccupation was shared by other writers of the time; the play entitled *The Mask and the Face*, that was popular around the time of the First World War, was written not by Pirandello but by Luigi Chiarelli.

The plays discussed in this chapter, spanning a ten year period from the early 20s to the early 30s, all take up the question of the relativity of identity in different ways. *Henry IV* (1922) and *Diana and Tuda* (1927) show the darker side of the search for an identity that can be grasped and held, *As You Want Me* (1930), *Finding Oneself* (1932) and *When One is Somebody* (1932) are more cynical than tragic, but all five plays are structured around the crisis of an individual. Whether this can be read as a sign of increasing introspection on Pirandello's part, as his love-affair with Fascism moved out of its first euphoric stage, is a matter for speculation, but it is clear that the interest in satirizing bourgeois society gives way in these plays to a concern for the personal struggles of his protagonists. The commentator figures, such as Laudisi, Lodovico Nota or Diego Cinci, are less apparent, and the emphasis is on the relationship between the inner self and the projected outer selves.

Roger Oliver, in his book on Pirandello's theatre, discusses the way in which Pirandello uses the term *costruirsi* (to build oneself, to create oneself). This process of creating a self stems from the need to cover the incongruities that the humourist is seeking to expose, and Oliver points to the irony in Pirandello's choice of a title for his collected dramatic works, *Naked Masks*. The mask, Oliver claims succinctly, can be used in different ways:

> A mask can be a fiction created as part of a *costruzione*, of which the person using it is constantly aware. It can also be a fiction that comes to be believed in by the individual as his true reality. A mask can also be a construct that is forced upon the person by society in order to protect itself, especially if that person's behaviour threatens to endanger the established order.[1]

'Henry IV'

Henry IV is probably the best known of Pirandello's plays, and has been more frequently performed in Italian and in

103

English than even *Six Characters*. Written for Ruggero Ruggeri, the role of Henry is the greatest male part in Pirandello's oeuvre, and the play has frequently been compared with *Hamlet*. Discussing his staging of the play in 1967, the year of the celebration of the centenary of Pirandello's birth, Vaclav Hudecek, the Czech director, talks about the play:

> The desire to take one's bearings in this absurd world, ceaseless efforts to draw up the map of oneself and the mental dispersion resulting from the conglomerate of these confused sentiments characterise the man of the second half of the twentieth century. All this can be found in Henry.[2]

The plot of *Henry IV* is well-known even to those who may never have read or seen the play. Some twenty years before the action begins, a group of young Italian aristocrats had staged a masquerade, where each guest had elected to come as a famous historical character. One of these young men had chosen to come as the Emperor Henry IV, carefully studying the background to his role to ensure greater authenticity. During the masquerade he had fallen from his horse, hit his head and, as a result of the cerebral damage caused by the fall, had awoken suffering from the delusion that he was indeed Henry IV. Being of a sufficiently wealthy background for private nursing to be arranged, the young man was shut away in a country villa instead of an asylum, and in order to humour his delusion, the villa was decorated to look like a medieval castle, with successive servants and nurses dressed in costumes of the time of Henry IV.

The play starts with a joke. The latest one in a series of servants, Bertoldo, has just arrived at the villa in the wrong costume, having confused his Henries and believing he has come to the court of Henry IV of France. His arrival provides a means of filling in the details of Henry's madness for the audience, and shortly after this introduction, visitors are announced. The young Marquis di Nolli, Henry's nephew, his fiancée Frida, her mother Matilde and her mother's lover, Belcredi, have come to visit Henry, bringing with them a psychiatrist. The servants insist that they dress up before meeting Henry, and as they prepare to be received into his presence, further details come to light. We learn that there was once something between Matilde and Henry at the time of the masquerade, in which both she and Belcredi were involved, and we learn also that Belcredi views Henry's madness with a certain cynicism. Their uneasiness as they wait for Henry creates a sense of tension, and when he does finally appear, towards the end of Act I, his entrance comes as a shock. For Henry is now nearly fifty years old, pallid and with greying hair, but he has dyed parts of his hair yellow and is heavily made up in an attempt to hide the ravages of time. He looks, in short, the perfect picture of a madman. In the scene which follows, however, his madness is harder to pin down, and he seems at times to be playing with his distinguished visitors, making them more ill at ease than ever.

Act II begins with the Visitors discussing their impressions of Henry. The Doctor talks in learned terms about madness, but neither Matilde nor Belcredi, for different reasons, is convinced that he is mad at all. The Doctor devises a plan which, he hopes, will cure Henry by jolting him into the twentieth century. Matilde's daughter, Frida, who looks now as her mother did twenty years before, is to dress up in her costume. There are two life-size portraits in the room, one of Henry and one of

Matilde at the time of the masquerade. Frida and Di Nolli will stand in front of the portraits, and when Henry appears Frida will step down out of the frame, as it were. This plan, according to the Doctor, will shock Henry into an awareness of normal time.

While the Visitors are offstage preparing for this moment of truth, Henry reveals to his group of retainers that he is not mad at all. Some years previously he had found his madness 'cured', but has gone on living as Henry IV because he has chosen to do so. The sane Henry reflects bitterly on the irony of madness – madmen 'construct without logic', they live apart from the terror that sane people face, the terror of knowing that nothing in life can ever be fixed and that time destroys everything. Henry achieves tragic stature in this second act, in contrast to the shallowness of the retainers who do not understand the profundity of what he says to them.

The crisis comes in Act III, a brief act which moves at a rapid pace. Frida plays her part and steps out of the picture frame, and Henry is goaded into telling the visitors about his years of madness and sanity, how he has lived twenty years shut away in a masquerade that has become his reality. This is my life, he tells them, but even as he does so he is forced to recognize the inevitability of the passing of time. No longer able to recognize the aging Matilde, he seizes Frida in a sudden vain attempt to hold on to the love of his imagination. Belcredi intervenes, shouting that Henry is not mad and cannot hide behind a mask of madness. In a wild gesture of retaliation, Henry stabs him. This gesture confirms everyone's belief that he is mad and the play ends with Henry condemned to live out the rest of his life as Henry IV, trapped forever in the guise of a madman. 'Here together . . . forever' are the last words of the play. Henry has stepped out of his role for an instant, but his action in that split second of time has forced him back into it, permanently.

Throughout the play, links are drawn between madness and acting. The madman, like the actor, is not bound by the laws of time, space and sequence as ordinary human beings are. In Act I, talking to Matilde, Henry reminds her of her attempts to disguise herself, comparing her actions with his own and pointing to the distinction between the image in the mirror and the individual's perception of herself – the mask and the face. Matilde must know that her make-up cannot alter the changes made by the passing of time; she makes up to see her reflected image become closer to the memory she has of her younger self, her idealized self-image. In this respect, she is as 'mad' as Henry, locked into the past and trying to relive it.

In Act III, after the Doctor's attempted cure, Henry again confronts Matilde with the significance of disguise. 'Who cares about clothes if he's really cured?' she asks, ignoring the elaborate role playing that has gone on for twenty years. In this dismissal she confirms Henry's worst fears – that his lost years are meaningless to the outside world. He tries to explain the importance of the robe he is wearing. His disguise is the caricature, he says, of life,

> that other masquerade, the one which continues every moment and in which we are the involuntary clowns (*pointing to Belcredi*)
> when, without knowing it, we mask ourselves as whatever we think we are

Belcredi is the only other person to understand something of what Henry is trying to say. Earlier, when the plan to cure Henry was being set up, Belcredi had argued against it, pointing out that it was not just a simple matter of twenty years' delusion. For Henry, trapped in that delusion, it is eight hundred years:

> For us, it's just twenty years, two costumes and a masquerade. But if, as you say Doctor, he's living there (*pointing to Frida*) with her, eight hundred years ago, I say the leap will leave him so giddy that when he lands among us . . . .

He is interrupted by the Doctor, who insists that Belcredi is wrong. Life can be taken up again, he argues, for like all the Searcher figures in Pirandello's plays, he believes that absolute truth *does* exist and that all he has to do is to find it. This belief in the absolute is repeatedly treated by Pirandello as a kind of madness, perhaps the greatest delusion of all. The irony of *Henry IV* is the irony of the essay 'On Humour': those declared by some to be mad because they do not conform to social norms are less 'mad' than those who believe in the existence of absolutes. Moreover, whatever their state of madness or sanity, all human beings are condemned to exist in a world of motion and time from which there is no escape. When he first appears, Henry talks about life in terms that recall the essay 'On Humour':

> we're all fixed in good faith in a splendid concept of what we are. But, Monsignor, while you're standing there so firmly, holding on tight with both hands to your sacred robes, something is slipping away out of the sleeves, slipping, slithering like a serpent – something you don't even notice. Life, Monsignor.

At this point in the play, however, everyone believes Henry is mad, so his words have no weight in the world of the

Visitors. Like the Fool in *King Lear*, or like Lear in his real madness and Edgar in his feigned madness, Henry is beyond social conventions and can say what he likes. The price for this freedom is that his words will not be heeded. When he stabs Belcredi, this can be seen as his last desperate attempt to show that he cannot be dismissed as a senseless lunatic, but all he succeeds in doing is to convince the others of his madness. Having created a world of security for himself, using the script provided by history, Henry's illusions are shattered. Like Leone Gala, in *The Rules of the Game*, Henry has tried to control the world he lives in, and like Leone Gala he is finally doomed to immobility. This is the heart of the tragedy: no-one can escape the inevitability of change and decay. Matilde may be a jealous, unhappy middle-aged woman, the Doctor may be a phony who puts his trust in the inadequate laws of science, and neither may have a choice in the matter, but when Henry is finally condemned to being the mad Emperor, it is because he consciously tried to play a part and create an illusion to spare himself greater pain.

Walter Starkie uses a musical image to describe the structure of the play:

> Like a theme ever recurring though the mazes of orchestration of a symphony, the idea of distance and time is repeated again and again in the play.[3]

Other themes recur through the play: the clash between the motion of life and the fixity of art, the relative freedom of the madman and the artist, the impossibility of ever judging sanity other than by arbitrary means. The play is not so rigidly structured around keywords as many of Pirandello's other plays, and is pinned to the character of Henry rather than to any other structural system. Silvio d'Amico rated this play very highly indeed. Writing in 1922, he argued that *Henry IV* had a breadth of vision unrivalled by any of Pirandello's other works, where the emphasis had been on the misery of the narrow world vision of petit bourgeois society, and in his letter to Ruggeri outlining the plot, Pirandello himself declared the play to be 'one of my most original ones'.

The question of the boundaries between madness and sanity is a recurrent theme in much twentieth-century art and literature, connected as the problem is to definitions of power and control. In *Madness and Civilisation*, Michel Foucault comments that

> the ultimate language of madness is that of reason, but the language of reason enveloped in the prestige of the image, limited to the locus of appearance which the image defines.[4]

Madness is the point of overflow, the moment when all supposed boundaries are swept aside. By choosing to write a play about madness, Pirandello again finds a way of exploring the ideas he had set out in his essay 'On Humour', and in dealing with the plight of one man, he is able to broaden the spectrum and present a bitterly tragic vision of the world. Henry's predicament is a sign of man's predicament, caught between structures and definitions in a world over which he has no control, no matter how he may delude himself into thinking that he might have.

'Diana and Tuda'

Diana and Tuda is one of the least frequently performed of Pirandello's plays. It was originally written for Marta Abba and the stage directions describing Tuda's

110

extraordinary beauty, as Leonardo Bragaglia has pointed out,[5] offer an idealized portrait of Marta Abba herself:

> She is young, magnificently beautiful. Thick, curly hair, done in the Greek style. Her mouth often has an expression of pain, as if everyday life had given it a twist of bitterness, but if she laughs, she is enveloped in a luminous gracefulness that seems to lighten everything and make her more alive.

The play is a reworking of the Pygmalion myth, where the love of an artist for the statue he has created is finally rewarded by the gods when the statue is turned into a living woman. It is easy to see how this myth might appeal to Pirandello, since it deals essentially with the dichotomy between art and life, but Pirandello uses the myth in a manner consistent with his particular vision, where the gods do not intervene to bring about a happy ending.

Described by Pirandello as a tragedy, the play deals with the way in which an obsessive view of art can destroy the forces of life from which all art originates. Sirio Dossi, a sculptor, is carving a statue of Diana, using Tuda, a beautiful, energetic woman, as his model. Once the statue is completed and his life's work fulfilled, Sirio proposes to kill himself. He lives only for his statue and life without it is meaningless for him. Tuda, on the other hand, is brimming over with exuberance and is strongly attracted to Sirio as a man. Concerned that she might hinder his work by going off to pose for other artists, Sirio proposes marriage to her: he offers her wealth, social position and complete freedom (he already has a mistress, Sara) provided she agrees to work only for him. Tuda weighs up this cold-blooded proposal and decides to accept.

In Act II, the effects of married life begin to tell on her.

She surrounds herself with dress-makers and milliners, lives a life of great luxury and, as she flippantly tells Sara whom she meets by chance, is ruining Sirio with her extravagances. Tuda and Sara are uneasy and hostile with each other, and Sara taunts Tuda with her promise of fidelity. If Tuda were to model for anyone else, such as Sirio's rival Caravani, for instance, Sara claims that it would be 'goodbye house, goodbye clothes, goodbye furs', implying that Tuda is Sirio's paid servant. Goaded by this, Tuda declares that she *will* model for Caravani to prove her independence, and tells Sara to go and announce this decision to Sirio. The act ends with Tuda leaving with Caravani.

The middle ground, between Sirio's coldness and Tuda's passion, is personified in the figure of Giuncano, an aging sculptor who is unable either to create in his own right or to express his feelings adequately. Giuncano is the warning voice in both acts, in a manner similar to Belcredi in *Henry IV*, urging moderation, pointing out that time passes quickly, telling Tuda that life itself is a trap in which all mankind is caught. The irony is that Giuncano is hopelessly in love with Tuda and deeply conscious of a sense of waste. Sirio is married to Tuda and yet rejects her as a woman, Giuncano desires her but is too old to be loved in return.

In Act III the sense of tragedy intensifies. Giuncano and Sara discuss Tuda, who has disappeared. Sara defends her part in causing the breach between Tuda and Sirio, revealing to Giuncano details of her own personal unhappiness. Then Tuda comes back, but as a changed woman. She is harder now, with the brightness of her first appearance dulled, and she insists that Sirio must finish the statue that he has been unable to work on since she left. Immortalized in the statue, she declares that her real life *is* the statue, and that she needs Sirio as much as he needs her. The ideal beauty that is her own image will not be subjected to any processes of decay in the statue, and she will remain alive and idealized in Sirio's creation. In the final moments of the play, as she cries out to Sirio to take what life remains to her and 'seal it into your statue', she tries to embrace the statue, her other self. Sirio moves to prevent her and in a moment of rage, Giuncano intervenes and stabs him. With Sirio lying dead, unable ever to work on his statue again, Tuda feels that she has been annihilated. Her final words, on which the play ends are a statement of her hopelessness: 'Now I am nothing . . . nothing at all'.

If *Henry IV* is the tragedy of a man taken over by the mask he has put on, *Diana and Tuda* is the tragedy of a woman whose life-energy has drained into the statue that is an image of herself. Early in the play, when Sirio Dossi is trying with great difficulty to get Tuda to stand still so that he can work, Giuncano warns her almost playfully about the danger of fixity. Tuda asks him if he thinks she is beautiful:

GIUNCANO: Yes, dear – Dead.
TUDA: How do you mean, dead?
SIRIO (*shouting*) Stand still.
TUDA: But you said dead . . . .
GIUNCANO: Precisely, because he wants you to keep still like that.

Later in the same scene Sirio talks about the eternal life that statues possess, but Giuncano refuses to accept this view:

What do you mean 'alive', if being alive means dying

every second, changing every second – and that thing doesn't die and doesn't change either? It's dead for ever there in its life-likeness. You give it life if you look at it for a moment.

Diana and Tuda is one of Pirandello's clearest statements about the dilemma facing the artist who seeks to freeze life in the form of a created work. (This play also squares with Fascist ideology, since Pirandello seems to be saying that a notion of art which seeks to glorify itself at the expense of life-forces is sterile.) Yet at the same time he recognizes the artist's need to try and create something that will have eternal life. In Act I Giuncano dreams about breathing life into statues, like Pygmalion. His impossible dream is diametrically opposed to the vision of Sirio who, for his part, wants to create the single, perfect work and sees himself as above other human activities:

> . . . what he calls 'living'
> (*to Giuncano, angrily*)
> what is it? travelling, like my brother does now? gambling, loving women, having a beautiful house, dressing well, listening to all the usual things, doing all the usual things? living for living's sake?

Sirio, however, is not so much anti-life as pro-art in an extreme idealistic way. He models from life in order to create the perfect image, a position that we might readily expect from a D'Annunzian protagonist. But through the vitality of Tuda, whose life is wasted by Sirio's idealism, the sympathy of the audience is swung against the sculptor. Moreover, the figure of Giuncano, the aging humourist who can see both sides of the coin, further moves our sympathies towards life (Tuda) rather than the abstraction of art (Sirio).

Throughout the play Giuncano is given a series of speeches involving the central motif of *sight*. *Cecità* (blindness) is the keyword, which takes on greatest prominence in the closing moments of the play. When Giuncano first appears he tells Sirio about the pleasure he experienced that morning at the sight of coloured parakeets enjoying the sunshine on their balconies. Sirio is momentarily taken aback – he cannot understand the point of this conversation. Giuncano explains:

> Because now I can see. That's why I've gone mad, as you said. If you only knew how many things I couldn't see before.

At the end of the play when he has killed Sirio, Giuncano can only repeat that one word *cecità* (blindness), and the ambiguity of this ending gives rise to speculation as to what Pirandello was actually trying to say. The play is about blindness on many levels – Sirio is blind to life and love, to all that Tuda has to offer, Tuda is blind to Giuncano's passion, since his age leads her to see him as a father-figure rather than as a lover. When she tries to embrace Sirio's statue, her 'other self', it is as though she has become infected with Sirio's disease and now is blinded in turn to life itself. Giuncano, the only one who *can* see, has nevertheless killed Sirio in a moment of blind rage, similar to that experienced by Henry when he stabs Belcredi. Blindness, the play seems to be saying, is endemic to the human condition.

The figure of the humourist, able to stand on the side and wryly comment on the follies of mankind, has undergone a major change in *Diana and Tuda*. Giuncano may be able to see more clearly, but he is also involved in the destinies of the two protagonists and cannot set himself apart to watch. This tendency for all characters to be involved in the action shows another way in which Pirandello was beginning to move away from a more satirical drama, and it also shows a deepening of his increasingly pessimistic vision. Laughter in *Henry IV* and *Diana and Tuda* is short-lived and bitter and was to be even less evident in plays written in the late 20s and early 30s. No-one is exempted from the tragic events of *Diana and Tuda*; Sara, Sirio, Giuncano and Tuda all lose whatever hopes of happiness and fulfilment they may have once had. In his last main speech before the murder of Sirio, Giuncano relates their tragedy to the fate of humanity. He tells Sirio that he should have married a cardboard dummy:

> It would have stayed there fixed for you, just as you wanted – for your statue, which is fixed too, just as it should be. Time without age: the most terrifying thing of all.
> SIRIO: What do you mean, without age?
> GIUNCANO: Age, which is time when it becomes human – time when it suffers – like us, made of flesh.

Time, Giuncano claims, which is synonymous with pain, has changed Tuda into a creature unlike the perfect beauty of the statue, and this change has come about through suffering. Giuncano is voicing the favourite Pirandellian concept of life as movement, with the inevitability of unhappiness caused by the inexorable passing of time.

'As You Want Me'

Three years after *Diana and Tuda*, Pirandello wrote *As You Want Me* for Marta Abba. This play was more successful than *Diana and Tuda*, largely due to Marta Abba's performance which was widely acclaimed. Although not frequently performed, it was nevertheless made into a film in 1933 starring Greta Garbo and Erich von Stroheim, directed by George Fitzmaurice, with the title *As You Desire Me.*

As You Want Me is a powerful play, which again raises questions about Pirandello's political stance. The action in the play takes place ten years after the Great War, and is set in Berlin and Udine. The events chronicled through the three acts derive from a ghastly sequence of happenings that took place during that war; the climax of the play fuses the past and the present in a grim reminder of the inhumanity of human beings in the face of suffering. What emerges clearly from this play, perhaps more so than from any of the plays discussed in this chapter, is the loneliness of the individual trapped in his or her fate. Pirandello seems to be implying that the individual must always suffer alone, regardless of any socio-political system. The mood of this play is a long way from that of the euphoric public listening to Mussolini in the Piazza Venezia. Behind the mask of competence and coherence is a face twisted by despair.

The first act takes place in the exotically furnished home of Carl Salter, a writer. The woman he lives with, referred to throughout in the stage directions as *L'Ignota* (the Unknown Woman), is an actress and entertainer. The third member of the household is his daughter, Mop, described in curiously strong terms:

> *Her hair is cut like a boy's and when we see her face, it is characterized by a slightly repulsive ambiguity and, at the same time, by a profoundly disturbing hint of tragedy.*

117

The play opens on an odd note. Mop is sitting in a chair crying, and Salter comes on in a state of great agitation, fingering a small revolver which he hastily puts in his pocket. Almost immediately there is the sound of a quarrel offstage, and the Unknown Woman enters surrounded by four young men all drunkenly trying to seduce her. She is defended by Boffi, who finally manages to throw them all out.

This striking opening sets the tone of the play and establishes a sense of decadence. Through this world of corruption, symbolic of innocence lost, the Unknown Woman will emerge, in spite of all that happens to her, as the only strong character. Salter and Mop are both in love with her, but she is contemptuous of them. 'This could only happen to me,' she tells Boffi, early in the play, 'they're actually jealous of one another.' But in spite of her contempt, she continues to live with them in what she describes as madness and corruption. Behind the gaiety and frantic pursuit of pleasure, there is a tormented soul struggling to assert itself. In Act I, talking to Boffi, the Unknown Woman frankly admits to her despair:

> What do I want? I want to get away from myself, certainly – not to have to remember anything – I want to empty life out of me. Yes, listen – a body – to be just a body . . . do you think you own your own body? does it look like you? . . . I don't feel myself any more, I don't want myself any more – I don't know anything, I don't know myself. My heart beats, and I don't know about it, I breath and I don't know about it – I don't know anything about living any more – I'm a body, a nameless body waiting for someone to take me.

Boffi has come, in fact, to offer her a name to put to that

118

body. He has come to her from Udine, where Bruno Pieri, his friend lives. During the war, ten years earlier, Pieri's villa had been broken into by invading soldiers, who raped his wife, Cia, and carried her off. Pieri had assumed that she was dead, but is now convinced that the Unknown Woman is really his lost Cia, and has sent Boffi to bring her home. The Unknown Woman hears Boffi out, and does not commit herself with any statements, except to comment that if Pieri believes he will find his wife after ten years as he previously knew her then he must be mad. Salter, distraught at the thought of her going, shoots himself, but bungles it and the act ends with the Unknown Woman, alone on stage, torn between a sense of duty to Salter and a desire to take up the chance of a new life elsewhere.

By Act II, she has made her decision and gone to Udine. Two old people, Zio Salesio and Zia Lena, study the Unknown Woman in order to convince themselves of the truth of what they see. The Unknown Woman has deliberately dressed herself up in the same clothes as a large portrait of Cia hanging on the wall, and she treats the old peoples' comments with ironic humour:

> This is quite an act you're putting on, uncle, about how you see me and how Lena sees me and how anybody can recognize someone who disappeared ten years ago, when the entire enemy army must have marched over her!

Living in her new role, Cia runs into all kinds of problems, the chief of which is the continued doubt about the *truth* of her identity. The search for verifiable evidence that will irrefutably declare her to be Cia, is similar to the search of the Neighbours in *Right You Are*, with the

119

difference that in Cia's case it is her personal freedom that is at stake. The culmination of Act II is the point where Cia confronts Bruno Pieri and gently shows him that he lacks faith in her. She has given him back his greatest desire, she tells him, and in the giving has wiped out her years of decadence, returning as the pure wife:

> Poor Bruno, poor, poor Bruno, so worried about these documents that can be presented as proof! Relax! I am Cia – renewed! You want so many things! I didn't ask for anything coming here, not even for the right to live my own life . . . .

Salter, meanwhile, claims to have found the 'real' Cia, a patient in a Viennese mental hospital, and Act III opens with all Cia's relatives waiting for the arrival of this second woman. Bruno tries to explain why he is unable to keep faith with the woman he has just accepted back as Cia, arguing feebly that once suspicions begin they cannot be stopped. When the mad woman appears she can only utter one word 'Le–na', but Salter seizes on this as proof – she must be referring to Zia Lena who brought Cia up. Boffi tries to intervene, but forces are in motion that he is unable to control. Not even the arrival of the Unknown Woman and the poignant contrast between the two women can allay the doubts that have arisen. The Unknown Woman continues, as she has always done, to press no claim, even pointing out that Cia might just as well be the mad woman. Although she, the Unknown Woman, looks like Cia, that resemblance might itself be evidence that she cannot be Cia because no-one could look the same after ten years' suffering:

> Only if you believe – when you want to believe – that

something is clear, are you able not to think (or refuse to think) that being like this, the same, is evidence *against* me. And then – why not? – Cia really could be this poor woman precisely because she shows no sign of a resemblance at all.

The Unknown Woman goes on to give graphic details of the horrific fate that overtook Cia ten years earlier, and as she tells her story the others gradually come to believe that she must be Cia. But it is too late: the Unknown Woman has asked for faith and not received it. Caught up in the need for precise proof of her identity, Bruno Pieri and the family at the villa have shown her the gap that exists between them.

As the play ends, the Unknown Woman tells them she has decided to go *back* to Berlin with Salter, throwing one last mocking challenge to them as she leaves:

THE UNKNOWN WOMAN: One more thing! Don't forget to ask her sister if this poor creature has a birthmark on her thigh . . . .

DOCTOR: Yes, a mole . . . .

THE UNKNOWN WOMAN: A red one? Is it raised up? Does she really have one?

DOCTOR: Yes, it's raised up, but it's not red, it's black, and not quite on her thigh . . . .

THE UNKNOWN WOMAN: In this diary it says: 'red and raised up, on the thigh – like a red beetle.'
(*To Bruno*)
See? It must have gone black . . . it must have moved too – but she has one! That's further proof that she's Cia! – Believe that she is!

The play ends with the mad woman repeating her

monosyllable, as the family stand around helplessly, listening to Cia's car drive away.

When she chose to direct this play in the 1980/81 season of the Teatro Stabile di Torino, Susan Sonntag tried to give a feminist reading to the part of Cia. In her analysis of that production, Jennifer Stone[6] points out that such a reading restricts the scope of the play. Although Pirandello shows the same bourgeois moral stance regarding the right of women to control their own sexual needs that emerges so often in his plays, *As You Want Me* is 'an anatomy of power and powerlessness, which is not always gender specific.' The figure of the Unknown Woman provides a means of attacking belief in the singleness of identity, and in the struggle between faith and reason the Unknown Woman wins a moral victory. She alone can see the futility of wanting things to remain as they are, and she can also see how the individual is constructed by the way in which others perceive her.

There is no keyword in this play, but the use of names functions in a similar way. All three acts end significantly with references to the identity provided by a name. In Act I, the Unknown Woman, alone on stage repeats the line 'A body with no name, no name'. In Act II she repeats the name, Cia, and the stage directions are quite explicit:

BRUNO (*almost pleading*) Cia . . . .

THE UNKNOWN WOMAN (*pausing, turning, very calm and in a tone of voice that is asserting something about which there can be no doubt*) Yes . . . well . . . Cia.

At the end of Act III, with the Unknown Woman gone, the mad woman babbles 'Le–na' and Zia Lena whispers 'unbelievingly' 'Cia'. Names lose their weight without faith and become meaningless.

The bleakness of this play derives not only from the contrast between a belief in fixity and the harshness of life that will allow nothing to be fixed. *As You Want Me* is set in a time of decadence and anarchy, and throughout the play references are made to the ugliness and brutality of German culture. Cia was raped and abducted by German soldiers, the Unknown Woman lives with the coarse Carl Salter and his homosexual daughter and earns her living as a nightclub performer in Berlin. Yet when she tries to live in Italy, in the villa that Bruno Pieri has rebuilt, the lack of faith in her drives her away once again. It is tempting to draw parallels between the plight of the Unknown Woman and Pirandello's own situation, living in self-imposed exile in Berlin and feeling universally unwelcome. The isolation of the individual condemned to live as an outsider becomes especially poignant when we consider Pirandello's attempts, a few years earlier, to become part of a group, both by joining the Fascist party and by setting up his own theatre company. The tone that characterizes the plays discussed in this chapter came increasingly to highlight the individual's pain, rather than the individual's protest.

'Finding Oneself'

This play was also written for Marta Abba, and was first performed in Naples in 1932 with her in the leading role. It was not a great success and remains one of the least well-known of Pirandello's theatrical works. Giudice's biography contains an anecdote about a performance of *Finding Oneself* in Helsinki in 1933 where Pirandello was present in the audience, and a young Finnish writer commented that 'We had the impression . . . that Pirandello was no longer a contemporary of ours . . . .'

What emerges clearly from a consideration of *Finding*

Oneself is a sense of the way in which Pirandello had come to dissolve conventional plot structures. Even in *Six Characters* or *Each in His Own Way* there is a plot line in which different stages in the action have clearly definable functions, but Pirandello moved increasingly towards a more abstract kind of theatre where plot was of secondary importance. The plot of *Finding Oneself* is full of unexplained sidelines, and one has the feeling that this thin plot line only exists in order to allow the protagonist to play a series of powerful, yet loosely connected scenes. The play is centred upon an actress, Donata Jenzi, whom we first encounter in Act I as a guest at a wealthy friend's villa. Before her first appearance, fellow guests discuss her past and argue also about the meaning of acting, in a superficial examination of the question of an actor's 'sincerity'. When Donata appears, she dominates the others through a series of long speeches, in which she claims that as an actress she is never herself but is the character that she has chosen to play:

> I tell you that I live the life of my character from the time I'm playing her. I am not myself.

Donata extends the discussion still further by talking about the pain such dislocation can cause. When a play ends, she is jolted abruptly back out of one life into the squalor of the dressing room and the exhaustion after a performance, no longer aware of who she really is. The keyword *trovarsi*, (finding oneself) which is taken up in the title of the play, recurs throughout Donata's speeches.

While staying at the villa Donata meets Elj Nielsen, a young Swede with whom she falls deeply in love, and in Act II they are seen living together. However, it is obvious from the start that their relationship is doomed. Elj sees life as freedom of movement, symbolized by the sea to which he constantly refers and to which he ultimately returns. Donata, on the other hand, sees life as a process in which she is inextricably bound by certain forces, the strongest of which is her own inner compulsion to fulfil herself as an artist. Elj wants her to give up the theatre and stay with him, but in the clash between love for a man and love for her art, the human part loses.

Act III opens with a distraught Elj deciding to leave Donata, since he is unable to cope with her public success on stage. When Donata arrives, fresh from her triumphant performance, he has already gone. Her friends try to console her, but she needs no such help. In a series of powerful speeches she tells them what she has discovered about herself: in finding the extent of her own capacity for love, she also found that she was in danger of being consumed by it. The process of finding herself through love only revealed a further possibility of losing that self. Loving Elj meant denying the part of herself that had chosen the theatre as a profession. The price was too high, and, as Donata says, finding oneself means ultimately being alone with oneself. The one compensation for that loneliness is the human imagination, and in the final scene of the play Donata sits alone, running through her part, and summons up, in a way that recalls the summoning of Madame Pace in *Six Characters*, 'true, living phantoms' to perform with her. The play concludes with Donata's assertion that:

This is true . . . and nothing's true at all . . . . The only thing that's true is the need to create and create oneself. And then, only then, can one find oneself.

Bragaglia sees the play as being about the conflict between

love and art, between human feelings and emotions and the almost superhuman vocation of the artist. Certainly this conflict does underlie the play to a large extent, but the balance is heavily weighted on the side of art. The unreality of Elj, the Swedish sailor, is made plain from the outset; his opposition to Donata's stage career emerges in Act III as petty jealousy, when he complains that she behaves on stage in the same way that she behaved in private with him, thus 'betraying' the exclusivity of their love. Donata dominates the play from start to finish: intellectually and emotionally she towers above the other characters who are merely foils for her complex speeches.

Two major shifts in Pirandello's writing can be discerned from a play like *Finding Oneself*. The first is the heavy stress laid on an ideal of art, on art as an almost metaphysical concept, beyond and above life. This is in marked contrast to the way in which the dichotomy between art and life was presented as a clash between fixity and motion in plays such as *Henry IV* and *Diana and Tuda*. The masks that Donata wears elevate her to an almost mystical status. She is not on the same level as other human beings.

The second clear line is an extension of what was beginning to emerge some years earlier, the way in which the moral value system of the play is determined by a woman. Donata's refusal to allow her love for Elj to become the centre of her life is a strong statement about a woman's need for personal freedom. Pirandello seems to have shifted his ground, from attacking the restrictions of bourgeois marriage to showing women struggling for a valid alternative, even if that means solitude and isolation. It is a startlingly advanced attitude and not one which squares with the Kinder, Kirche, Küche ideology of Fascism at all.

'When One is Somebody'

One year after *Finding Oneself*, a play closely linked to it in form and content was performed in San Remo, directed by Marta Abba, who also played the leading female role of Veroccia. Because Pirandello had failed to persuade an Italian company to take the play, however, the first performance was some two months earlier in Buenos Aires. *When One is Somebody* is another loosely structured piece that examines the relationship between the feelings and needs of the individual and the demands of art. In this play, which may be seen as a companion piece to *Finding Oneself*, the protagonist is a man, an aging writer, and more than one critic has noted the autobiographical parallels. Bragaglia is quite explicit: 'Once again we have an autobiographical play, about revolt and dissatisfaction.' Pirandello wrote to his daughter on 18 March 1933 saying that the play was the one he cared most about. He must have been all the more disturbed by the antagonistic reception that the play received from Italian critics when Marta Abba took it out on tour.

By the time *When One is Somebody* was performed, Pirandello's popularity at home and abroad had peaked and begun to decline. The vogue of Pirandellism was past. When he wrote his most famous works in the 1920s, they had the hard, bright edge that appealed to the post-war mood, but ten years later, with a world-wide economic recession, the picture looked very different. Pirandello's theatre had made demands on an audience in the early 20s that could no longer be made in the 30s. Moreover, the growing popularity of the cinema was a fact to be reckoned with. In 1929 Pirandello wrote an article entitled 'Will the Talking Film do away with Theatre?' ('Se il film parlante abolirà il teatro'), stating his refusal to accept the growing belief that theatre was a dying form. The cinema, he claimed, had been of universal appeal when it was *silent*, but with the advent of the talking film the silent actors would have to be replaced by actors used to speaking on stage. This would, in effect, strengthen the theatre rather than weaken it and would lead to the growth of national film industries instead of international ones. The key to the salvation of the theatre is therefore spoken language.

In *When One is Somebody*, the protagonist is a man whose public reputation has been created out of his abilities with language. The protagonist, who has no name and is referred to in the stage directions as ***, is a poet, with an international reputation. The fame he enjoys has become a kind of prison, for he is constantly pursued by admirers and is forced to write in accordance with the expectations of his public. Fame for *** is a mask behind which he is trapped. As he himself puts it in Act I:

The great man walks past and they fix you. They're stiff as posts, and they make you the same. They recall you to your 'fame' –you're a 'statue'.

The statue may have desires, ambitions, projects that he would like to pursue for his own sake, but since he is public property he is not allowed any personal space at all.

Before the action of the play begins *** has tried to break out of his prison. He has fallen in love with a young Russian girl, Veroccia, and as a result has written passionate, exciting new poetry, published under the pseudonym Delago. Delago is hailed as the great poet of youth, and as three young admirers declare in Act I, he is the voice of hope. But the forces binding *** within his mask prove too powerful to resist. In Act I we see ***

briefly happy with Veroccia, who is cutting his hair in a new youthful style, but when his predatory family arrive, eager to see him receive a prestigious literary award, *** gives up his dream. The stage directions stress his *public* image – 'even his hair seems to have grown back again'. ***'s decision to give up his new-found love follows the realization that the secret of his pseudonym is nearly out, and once the truth is known he will have nowhere left to hide:

> I'm not a Nobody, I'm SOMEBODY, I've told you that. 'I am as I am for everyone' and I can't be anyone else. If I reveal myself as Delago, it'll be over, he'll become one of my masks, don't you see that? A mask of youth that I put on as a joke.

The act ends with *** making a stately exit, described in vivid terms in the stage directions as being stiff and stone-like, the image of the walking statue, while Veroccia shouts definantly 'Viva Delago'.

Act II opens with ***'s dream of himself in his musty study. The images of some of Italy's greatest poets, Dante, Ariosto, Foscolo and Leopardi appear to him, but do not speak and only make negative gestures. This sequence emphasizes the sterility of fame, the way in which an image of greatness sucks out the living energy of the artist. When *** receives a visit from the young critics of Act I, who now come to accuse him of inventing Delago as a joke on his readers, he protests again about the way in which his fame deprives him of life:

> A joke! What a joke! All you can see is the joke! It's so impossible for you to believe that I could still think I was alive and trying to get out this prison of myself. I'm

129

shut in! Walled up! And I'm suffocating, dying in it . . . .

There is still another stage to ***'s suffering. Veroccia arrives, with her sister and brother-in-law, all of whom still believe in ***'s right to freedom, and attacks him for what she sees as cowardice. In deciding to accept the title of Count, conferred on him by the State in recognition of his literary eminence, and in denying the truth of his *other* self, Delago, *** has betrayed her love. But *** is so far back in his prison that he cannot speak, and only when she has gone can he try to justify himself to an empty room. As the act ends, *** speaks his monologue on the relationship between fame, loss of identity, sterility and death, concluding with the lines:

It's true that when one is Somebody, one has to condemn oneself to death at a certain point and stay shut up, like this, guarding oneself.

As he speaks, the stage darkens and the four poets emerge from the gloom as stiff and cold as statues.

In Act III the party to honour *** takes place off stage, and events are recounted by a group of journalists and members of the family. Veroccia is prevented from going in, and as she watches, she cries out that he is dead, then leaves quickly. Her sister and brother-in-law try for the last time to persuade *** to drop everything and leave with them, but he cannot. The play ends with a set-piece, as *** stands on a marble dais to address his admiring public:

As he begins to speak in a clear, ice-cold voice, he pauses as if to find the strength to chip out his words, which appear in the form of an epigraph on the façade of the villa behind him as if carved in stone, even as he utters them:

***: YOUTH
    ANCIENT FABLE OF MEMORIES
    SHADOW THAT APPROACHES YOU
    SHADOW
    THAT GOES FROM YOU

No-one is aware of the appearance of the sculpted words. The silence must remain unbroken.
. . . When everyone has gone, *** sits on the great chair and in clear moonlight the façade of the villa slowly recedes. At the same time the great chair starts to rise above the stage, with *** still sitting rigidly, a statue of himself. This takes place in what must seem like an endless silence.

On 1 June 1930, writing to Marta Abba from Berlin about the troubled première of *Tonight We Improvise*, Pirandello described himself in the following terms:

Everywhere I am pursued by hatred. Perhaps it is only right that this should be so, that I should die this way, annihilated by the hatred of triumphant cowards, by the incomprehension of idiots. After all they are the majority. The catcalls of idiots and of my enemies would not hurt me if my spirit were still what it used to be. But I have lost even the pride of my isolation, the love of my disconsolate sadness. . . . My two staring eyes remain inexorably fixed, despairing, proud, tired, heavy-lidded with a pain that no-one will ever be able to understand or know.
A great absolute immobility.[7]

From the mad Emperor to the un-named writer frozen in the mask of his own public image, these five plays show up the tragic side of Pirandello, the playwright of tortured ideas. All the protagonists in the plays end up trapped and helpless and there is little comedy to be found in the explorations of their pain. Moreover, through all five plays runs the motif of thwarted or unrequited love – in *Diana and Tuda* and *When One is Somebody* a young woman is loved by an aging man, in *Finding Oneself* the lover cannot cope with Donata's professional needs and leaves her, in *Henry IV* the object of Henry's youthful love has become the haggard, aging Matilde, and in *As You Want Me* the young bride is destroyed and cannot be found again.

The greater pessimism in these plays is reflected in the use of a series of stage devices that often seem over-ingenious and sterile. As Pirandello moved away from tightly structured plots, with carefully contrived climaxes, balancing the farcical and tragic on a fine line, he came to rely more on lighting effects, strong stage pictures and props. In *Henry IV*, for example, the portraits function as key visual signs, like the statue in *Diana and Tuda*, the portrait of Cia, the portraits of *** and Delago. In *Finding Oneself* the boundaries between Donata's real-life world and the 'real' world of her art dissolve at the end of the play when characters materialize on stage. *When One is Somebody* has lengthy directions for scene changing while the action is in progress, and at the end of the play magic words appear on the wall of the villa and *** is raised up and suspended in space. The lighting instructions for all five plays are very detailed; in *Diana and Tuda* for example a screen allows for shadow play as Tuda poses for Dossi behind it.

The use of these devices shows two things; firstly, Pirandello was deeply fascinated by Expressionist techniques and continued his experiments with theatre form in many more plays than the theatre-in-theatre trilogy. Secondly, the unsystematic use of such devices reiterates the sense of disillusionment that emerges from the thematic material. Even though he was working tirelessly – in 1930, for example, he was writing *The Mountain Giants*, staging *Tonight We Improvise*, planning *When One is Somebody* – the lack of direction he obviously came to feel can be discerned in his writing. Marta Abba quotes from another of his letters, written on 29 March 1929 in which he declares:

If you fill your days with work, always more work, and permit no time, absolutely no time, for boredom and regrets, life will no longer seem so empty.

5
Myth and Fable

Of the four plays discussed in this chapter, one dates from the earliest period of Pirandello's theatre writing and the remaining three date from the later period, with *The Mountain Giants* still unfinished when Pirandello died in 1936. *Liolà*, published in 1917, was first performed in 1916. *The New Colony* was published in 1928 and performed in the same year, while *Lazarus* was performed and published in 1929. The two acts of *The Mountain Giants* were performed posthumously in 1937, and published in the following year.

Critics have tended to consider *Liolà* as one of Pirandello's Sicilian plays, linking it to such works as *Sicilian Limes* (Lumie di Sicilia), *Cap and Bells* (Il berretto a sonagli) and *Think it over, Giacomino*, a perfectly valid categorization if what is considered primarily is the use of dialect and re-creation of a typically Sicilian ambience. But *Liolà* is also an anti-realist play, set in an idealized Sicily with a protagonist whose frequent use of poetry and song gives the play a dream-like quality. It is that dream-world which provides the main link between the four plays discussed here, for all are plays about an imaginary alternative to the reality of everyday life and all are plays that leave the audience with a strong sense of uneasiness. Pirandello's world view did not include a utopian belief in an ideal society; although he embraced Fascism as a step towards a more stable social order, there is no attempt in his works to portray a model proto-Fascist society. Indeed, Pirandello always declared himself to be apolitical, stressing his desire to be seen as 'just an ordinary human being', and insisting that although he might hold a party card, in his writing he was outside politics. In his essay on *The Mountain Giants*, Nino Borsellino points out the fallacy of such a belief, arguing that although he might declare himself to be apolitical, Pirandello

> could not do without politics in the relationship between art and power, that is reflected in society as a failure to integrate the human and the civil in poetry. For this reason he transforms his sense of exclusion into an ascetic compensation that emerges as a rejection of society in favour of nature.[1]

This tendency to try and look beyond the society in which he lived towards an idealized nature is as marked in *Liolà* as it is in *The Mountain Giants*, and it is significant that Pirandello himself attached high importance to all these plays. There is a ritualized metaphysical dimension to these plays too, in spite of the overt anticlericalism that emerges.

In his essay 'Will the Talking Film do away with Theatre?' Pirandello makes reference to Evreinoff, author of *The Theatre in Life*, quoting Evreinoff's view that theatre consists of all nature, including plants and animals. Pirandello goes on to add that there can be absolutely no doubt at all that before it was a traditional literary form, theatre was a natural expression of life.

This view comes close to Evreinoff's own theory that in order to believe in gods, man had first to conceive of those gods and personify them in the way that an actor personifies the character he portrays. In short, says Evreinoff, 'man became first an actor, a player; and then came religion'.[2] It is easy to see how such a theory might have attracted Pirandello, since it seemed to reinforce his own ideas that theatre might indeed be said to come from *nature* rather than from the society organized by men, or rather, that theatre might be apolitical. But what emerges from the plays discussed in this chapter, in all of which Pirandello variously expounded his ideas of nature versus society, is the sheer untenability of such a position. Liolà dances with his illegitimate children and defies conventional morality, La Spera clings to her child as the evil of the world is swept away in the floodwaters, but the murder of Matteotti and the invasion of Abyssinia were part of the fabric of Pirandello's life. Nero may have loved music, but Rome burned down nevertheless.

'Liolà'

In a letter to his son Stefano in 1916 Pirandello describes his feelings about *Liolà*. Claiming that he wrote the play in two weeks as his summer holiday recreation, Pirandello continues

I think I told you already that the protagonist is a poet-peasant, drunk on sunlight, and that the whole play is full of songs and sunshine and is so light-hearted that it doesn't seem like one of my works at all.

Liolà was a great success, in spite of the difficulties that the audiences had with Sicilian dialect, and has been revived at frequent intervals. Vittorio de Sica played the leading role in 1942, and in 1961, on the 25th anniversary of Pirandello's death, he directed another successful revival at the Teatro Quirino, Rome. Of this revival, Giorgio Prosperi, writing in *Il Tempo*, noted that de Sica had managed to reveal the original bitterness of the play, and to hit a note that undercut the superficial level of farce and hilarity.

The play that lends itself to comparison with *Liolà* is Machiavelli's Renaissance comedy, *La Mandragola*, a tale of lust and deceit, in which a foolish old husband is gulled and cuckolded. The foolish Zio Simone is similarly deceived in *Liolà*, but he does not suffer alone and the play ends on a note of vindictiveness that is by no means comic. The plot of *Liolà* centres upon the activities and lifestyle of the protagonist. Liolà is a peasant who loves women, and whenever his various lovers give birth to unwanted children, he takes them under his protection and gives them to his mother, Zia Ninfa, to bring up. He first appears in the company of three of his children, whom he describes as three parts of himself:

This one is LI, this one's O and here's LÀ.
The three together make up LIOLÀ.

In contrast to Liolà's fecundity is Zio Simone, a wealthy old man who has married the girl Liolà once loved, Mita. Mita's tragedy is two-fold – not only is she married to Zio Simone who maltreats her, but she has been unable to bear him a child for the four years of her marriage. The idea of childlessness is introduced as soon as the play begins, with the village women talking about Mita and her plight, for in the context of the Sicilian village childlessness is seen as a curse. Mita's plight deteriorates in Act II, when Tuzza, a sharp-tongued girl who has turned down Liolà's offer of marriage, declares that Zio Simone, her uncle, is the father of her unborn child. Zio Simone is delighted by this proof of his virility, and the unscrupulous Tuzza and her mother plan to disinherit Mita in favour of the unborn child. The truth, of course, is that this baby is also Liolà's, and he offers to help Mita by fathering a child on her as well. Mita at first refuses, but finally agrees, and in Act III she breaks the news to Zio Simone that he is about to become the father of a legitimate heir. Tuzza has been outwitted – Zio Simone prefers to believe that he has fathered a child on Mita and so their marriage is strengthened. Tuzza tries vainly to stab Liolà, but only succeeds in wounding him. The play ends with Liolà, surrounded by his children once again, telling Tuzza that he will take care of her child too.

Liolà is presented as a life force, as a kind of satyr figure, who loves the sun and the land, and like both is primitively fecund. He constantly inveighs against the restrictions of men's laws – the conventions of marriage, bourgeois morality, the laws of property inheritance – and indeed the alleged amorality of the play caused it to be withdrawn from repertoire at the Teatro Alfieri in Turin when it first appeared. Liolà is outspoken about sex, unhypocritical about his own desires and the desires of the women he loves. He frequently speaks in verse, sings and dances, thus becoming a tangible sign of gaiety and energy whenever he is on stage.

In contrast to Liolà is the sour Zio Simone, rich and impotent. In a crucial speech in Act I Liolà sets out his own philosophy of life in defiance of Zio Simone's 'official' view:

> LIOLÀ: Just be thankful, Zio Simone, that nobody disinherits you.
>
> ZIO SIMONE: And is that what they should do then?
>
> LIOLÀ: Why not? They could impose a law like that tomorrow. Couldn't they? Look, there's a piece of land here. If you stand and look at it and don't do anything, what does your land produce? Nothing. Like a woman. She doesn't give you children. Fine. I come to your piece of land, I hoe it, fertilize it, dig a hole in it, chuck a seed in: then you get a tree. So who did the earth give that tree to? To me. Then you come along and say no, it's yours. And why is it yours? Just because the land's yours? But Zio Simone, does the land know who it belongs to? It gives its fruits to the person who works it over. You take it because you stand on it and the law backs you up. But laws could change tomorrow, and then you could be pushed away with one hand. But the land would still be there for me to throw a seed into and there you are: a tree starts sprouting.

Liolà's attacks on property rights and the sterility of the bourgeois Zio Simone resound with revolutionary fervour, but what sours the cheerful note of this play is its extreme anti-feminism. Liolà may be pro-life, but he is anti-women on all levels. Not only are women in this play reduced to mere sexual objects, with the virtuous Mita as a chattel belonging to her husband and forced to acquiesce to Liolà's proposition, but the redeeming virtue of motherhood is also devalued. Liolà hands his children over to be looked after by his long-suffering mother, and thinks nothing of suggesting to Tuzza that she should hand her child over as well. Women are thus child-bearing vessels, no more and no less. They are, as Liolà so succinctly points out to Zio Simone, land to be hoed and fertilized. Moreover, the groups of village women who gather throughout the play are caricatured as spiteful gossips who spend their time talking, professing a false modesty that belies their sexual instincts.

Since the advent of feminist criticism, it has become impossible not to read *Liolà* as a tasteless example of reactionary male chauvinism, and so evident are the unpleasant aspects of the play that it is no longer easy to read it as the 'breezy' satire described by Walter Starkie in his early study in English of Pirandello's work.[3] But it would be a mistake to allow the distasteful elements to dominate an appraisal of the play. What Pirandello seems to have done is to create a work in which, as Starkie puts it, he 'tried to rival the ancient spirit of the sixteenth century'. That he failed to do so is an indication of the essential flaw in his apolitical stance – for in the make-believe Sicilian village of *Liolà*, compromise and deceit ultimately triumph. What Liolà offers Mita is a chance to cheat her way to Zio Simone's money, what he offers Tuzza is a chance to give birth to a child and then reject her own motherhood by giving that child to him. The nastiness of such a solution cannot be disguised. Liolà is treated sympathetically in this play, all the more so because the female characters and Zio Simone are treated so unsympathetically, but his is ultimately a flawed position. Life, Liolà says, is enjoyment and love and fecundity, and one feels that Pirandello, in the world of the Great War, living with his paranoid wife, must have longed to believe such an idea. But ultimately Liolà's way is destructive – he degrades women, forces his mother to bring up his children, condemns those children to a motherless existence and incites others to lie and deceive. Man is a loving island, Liolà proclaims, but such a notion is as illusory as the world of the play.

The Myths

In addition to the theatre-in-the-theatre trilogy, Pirandello grouped together three more plays, under the heading of *modern myths*. These three are *The New Colony*, the social myth, *Lazarus*, the religious myth and *The Mountain Giants*, the myth of art. To these three, Bragaglia adds two more: the one-act play, *La Sagra del Signore della nave* (*The Festival of our Lord of the Ship*), 1925, and *La favola del figlio cambiato* (*The Changeling*), 1938, myths of temporality and maternity.

By using the term 'myth' Pirandello clearly set out to indicate that in these works he was trying to do something different. In an interview with Alberto Cecchi in 1928 Pirandello explained that he wanted to address all mortal creatures in his work. 'Tragedy,' Pirandello declared, 'is always mythical. It has its beginning and end on the stage. The origins of myths are these: the elementary events of earthly cycles, dawns, sunsets, births, deaths.'[4] Pirandello was moving towards a notion of theatre that would provide the audience not only with something to see and discuss, but with something to experience directly. In his theatre of myth, the *coup de théâtre* is overtaken by the idea of the miracle, which actors and audiences share alike. What Pirandello was aiming for was a transcendent theatre, where the debate between life and art that had dominated much of his earlier writing would be subsumed into a new, global experience-theatre. In his short but important piece on Pirandello's theatre of myth, Sandro d'Amico refers to Julian Beck of the Living Theatre who had declared *The Mountain Giants* to be the climax of Pirandello's metatheatre. For in this last of his myths, Pirandello had attempted to tackle the vast problem of the impossibility of communication *and* the impossibility of producing theatre; in this sense the myths should be seen as a culmination of Pirandello's play-writing career, rather than as a decline into para-religious senility. D'Amico also suggests that the myths

> probably arose out of a need to clarify his own work and to give it a unity with the themes already apparent in his preceding works, such as charity, motherhood, sacrifice and pain.[5]

The parallels with Julian Beck, Luis Valdez and, more obviously, Grotowski, to name but three major post-war theatre innovators, may serve to further stress the importance of Pirandello's myths. For perhaps even more radically than in his theatre trilogy, Pirandello was endeavouring to produce a new type of theatre, to add a dimension to the whole process of theatre making. That the myths were never popular and have been largely ignored by directors and critics is another matter. They remain to be rediscovered, and their significance is well summed up by Giovanni Sinicropi, when he states that

> Pirandello's endeavour as man and artist closes thus with the recognition of the impossibility of bridging the gap between art and life. The last act of his creation had aimed at crossing that abyss; and even though he managed to reduce it to a small size, easily covered at one jump, it could never be filled up. The leap into the irrational area of myth does not have to derive from a

sense of renunciation, but one of achievement, of a necessary completion of the artist's aspirations.[6]

'The New Colony'

When this play was first staged, at the Teatro Argentina in Rome in 1928, with Marta Abba in the role of La Spera, both Abba's performance and Pirandello's direction were heavily criticized. However, the play itself was considered to be good, and the reviewer in the *Corriere della sera* declared it to be the 'least melancholy and most hopeful play' of Pirandello's entire output.[7]

The New Colony is a very long play, having three acts and a Prologue, and has an extended cast list. Moreover, its staging requires both indoor and outdoor sets, and these factors have no doubt contributed to the scarcity of revivals. It is cumbersome to stage and expensive, and would require careful handling to hold the huge cast together. It has only been revived twice in Italy since the original staging.

The Prologue serves to introduce the main characters and to present the world of corruption from which they try to escape. The scene is set in Nuccio's tavern, and we are introduced immediately to a clash of wills between Padron Nocio, the local landowner and Tobba, an old fisherman. Padron Nocio emerges as a Brechtian villain, a symbol of the corruption of power and wealth, who accuses Tobba of putting crazy notions into his son Doro's head:

PADRON NOCIO: You shouldn't go messing around with my son's ideas . . . .

TOBBA: Who me?

PADRON NOCIO: Yes, you, talking to him about your island. May God sink the blasted thing!

TOBBA: (*as though he expected something different*) Oh, the island.
(*Smiling*)
The paradise of wicked men.

The idea of the island, of the place of refuge where the evils of the world can be avoided is thus introduced in the opening moments of the play. Later in the Prologue, when the dissatisfaction of the poor fishermen, who eke out their livelihood by smuggling and live in constant fear of the law, has reached its climax, the idea of the island is brought up again. This time it is introduced by La Spera, the local whore whose lover, Currao, is one of the smugglers. La Spera has not been brutalized by her existence as some of the men have been, and she still has enough spirit to want to escape. She suggests flight to Tobba's island, and when the others refer to the belief that the island will one day sink into the ocean, La Spera convinces them with her enthusiasm:

CURRAO: (*thinking*) Go back to the island?
LA SPERA: It'll be our liberation.
FILACCIONE: Right! when you sink under the sea with it.
LA SPERA: And where are you here? haven't you sunk low enough already? You couldn't sink any lower than here. But at least it'll be God that pushes you under instead of men even wickeder than you are. They're wickeder because they won't even let you come up for air for a second just to breathe.

The island the smugglers go to is a former penal colony that has been abandoned because it was said to be gradually sinking into the sea. But to the wretched people of the mainland, led by La Spera and Currao, the image of the island becomes one of hope (the name *Spera* means

hope), for here they plan to build a new society, freed from
the shackles of the previous one. As the Prologue ends, La
Spera appears holding her child, the baby son without
whom she will not leave, and tells the others that a miracle
has occurred – she is suddenly able to breastfeed her own
child. Tobba speaks the final words of the scene, warning
the company that this is truly a sign from God, an
indication that He will guide them and protect them, and
in the final tableau all kneel in prayer.

Act I is set on the island, and it is immediately apparent
that the promise of a new life has not been fulfilled.
Because La Spera is the only woman on the island, the
other men lust after her, and Currao, who has become
their leader, uses his relationship with her to assert his
power the others. La Spera, the despised local whore
in her previous life, is now the queen of the island, and her
joy of motherhood causes her to be reborn in moral terms:
she becomes a truly pure woman, the source of all positive
values in the new society. The quarrels between the island's
new colonists intensify, and when one of them dies of a
heart attack at the end of Act I, the tableau is in marked
contrast to the end of the Prologue. For as the man lies
dead, a symbol of the failure of the attempt to create a new
life, only some of them kneel. Belief in God has begun to
fade.

In Act II, the forces of disintegration receive new help
with the arrival of Padron Nocio from the mainland,
bringing with him other women, including his daughter,
Mita. Padron Nocio sets up a deal with Currao in an
attempt to share the control of the new colony. La Spera's
growing isolation is symbolized by the concluding
moments of the act, when she sits alone with her child,
refusing to accept solitude, telling the baby that they
belong to each other.

The deal between Padron Nocio and Currao involves the marriage of Currao with Mita and the necessary abandoning of La Spera. Confused and lonely, La Spera resists attempts to make her give up her child to Currao, who is claiming the rights of fatherhood; in the final climax of the play she tries to prevent what she believes is an attack on the life of Doro, the young boy she has befriended. With the coming of Padron Nocio, La Spera's new status has been destroyed, and she is again treated as a whore. Clinging to her child, a symbolic figure of love and charity, she is insulted by the crowd who urge Currao on to pull the baby out of her arms. In despair, La Spera cries out that if he takes the child from her, 'the earth will quake', and the force of her belief makes this happen. The play ends with the cataclysmic swallowing up of the island by the sea. Out of the total destruction that ensues, only La Spera is left, with her child. The play ends with the image of La Spera and the child alone above the flood waters.

The New Colony is a play about the corruption of society, a corruption that men carry with them wherever they go. But although the play ends with the great destructive flood, the figure of La Spera represents a belief in an ideal. For La Spera is an indication of the *possibility* of change and the mere existence of that possibility gives hope. In Act I, when Currao declares that he knows the child is his, La Spera voices her hopes that a new life really is possible:

> If it were really true that coming here and changing our lives means that we'll all become different people from what we used to be . . . .

In contrast to her hope, the others refer constantly back to the life they once knew, either because they resent the loss of certain things or because they resent the changes that have come about. Their grievances focus on La Spera, the living proof that change can take place; only because of her new found strength is she able to deal with the way in which her past immorality is thrown back at her. In an important scene with Currao in Act II, the contrast between the strength La Spera gains through change and Currao's fears of the past emerges most clearly. La Spera tells Currao that her strength comes from the innocent faith of her child, whose love makes the evils of her past life seem like a bad dream.

> CURRAO: But he'll find out . . . . Tomorrow he'll find out. . . .
> LA SPERA: I'll teach him what he needs to know.
> CURRAO: If only there weren't other people . . . .

But of course those other people do exist, and in the end Currao proves himself to be as corruptible as any of them. What remains untainted is La Spera's love and faith, and it is because of that love that in the final holocaust she is saved.

Unlike so many of his plays, which have bourgeois protagonists, the characters of *The New Colony*, like the characters in *Liolà*, are poor, low-life figures. The language used is rich and colourful, and their coarse vitality is explicitly portrayed, but they are presented as bestial figures, in dark contrast to La Spera whose Madonna-like image grows through the play. Whereas in *Liolà*, the world of the Sicilian village was used to give a sense of exuberance, in *The New Colony* the world of poor fishermen is used to show the depths of human degradation.

The New Colony lends itself readily to comparison with

Brecht's *The Caucasian Chalk Circle*, where mother-love also emerges triumphant in a world of corruption. But although there may be superficial similarities, the gap between the Fascist playwright and the Marxist playwright looms large. Brecht shows the crisis of society as deriving from class struggle and from unequal distribution of wealth and power, and his plays are not empirical but dialectic. In Brecht's play, as in Pirandello's, the audience is on the side of the female protagonist in her struggles against the forces that seek to crush her, but in Brecht's play the heroine wins through and keeps the child she has saved because she acts in accordance with her natural instincts of love, and the judge rules in her favour. Her solution is thus brought about *by* society and by its laws, whereas in *The New Colony* there is no such solution. La Spera is saved by an act of God, by a *deus ex machina* that sweeps away her tormentors. She is not saved by reason or by love, nor by any of the forces that should go to making a new society, but by a completely irrational act that supposedly has divine origins. In this final *coup de théâtre* the extent of Pirandello's lack of commitment becomes apparent: the final miracle is superhuman and only reinforces the image of man's helplessness. With such a world view, there can be no new society, for Pirandello's characters do not have the capacity to work out a solution for themselves.

'Lazarus'

The second of the myths, *Lazarus*, had its world première in Huddersfield in 1929,[8] and, after its appearance in Italy in the same year, caused considerable debate. Pirandello's earlier anticlerical stance had earned him some enemies in religious circles, and his new myth of religion did nothing to dispel the suspicion with which he was regarded.

The play takes its name from the character in the Bible who was brought back to life miraculously, through the faith of Christ. The Lazarus theme has fascinated artists and writers for centuries, but Pirandello added a new dimension to the story by telling it in contemporary terms. The central figure of *Lazarus* (though not the figure who dominates the action of the play) is Diego Spina, a wealthy man who sets himself rigidly puritanical standards of moral behaviour. Long before the action of the play begins, his over-zealousness had driven his wife Sara away from him, and after she left him Diego Spina refused to allow her access to her two children, Lucio and Lia. Sara has since fallen in love with Arcadipane, a peasant farmer, and has renounced her middle class life in favour of life with him and their children out in the country. The children left with Diego Spina have been strictly brought up, with the result that Lucio is studying to become a priest and Lia lives a repressed, unhealthy life in the confines of her father's home. The dichotomy is thus set up between the purity and health of Sara's country life, glorified by work and love, and the narrow dullness of Diego's home, surrounded by a high symbolic wall and dominated by the image of a crucifix with 'a hideous, bleeding painted Christ' upon it.

The story of the separation between Diego and Sara emerges gradually as the action progresses, for the play is very much about expurgation of the past. Diego Spina faces a crisis in his life that forces him to come to terms with the deficiencies in himself that drove his wife away and threatened to blight his children's lives, but that realization does not come until the final moments of the play. For during the course of the three acts, Diego dies and is resored to life, and it is this event that leads to his crisis. In Act I, Diego's death and resurrection are prepared for when Dr. Gionni returns to Lia her pet rabbit that he has brought back to life with an injection. Diego absolutely refuses to accept this, arguing that it cannot possibly be true and that the rabbit must have been alive. He cannot admit anything that threatens his ordered universe; the irrational idea of resurrection is one to be immediately discarded. But later in Act I something else happens to disturb Diego's world: Sara arrives, to tell him that their son Lucio is with her, having decided to abandon the priesthood. Diego is horrified, both by what he sees as her presumption in daring to enter his house, and by the news of Lucio's decision. He demands to know the reasons for Lucio's actions, and Sara explains in language that returns us to the main theme of the play:

> SARA: He came to get to know me again.
> DIEGO: (*amazed*) To get to know you again?
> SARA: Yes, and to be born again, through me. To be born again through me, his mother, that's what he said.

Overwhelmed by his own feelings, Diego rushes out and blindly runs into a car. He is brought back into the room, and the act ends with the doctor pronouncing the single word *Morto* (dead).

In Act II there is a shift to the idyllic country setting of Sara's home where the bulk of the action consists of a dialogue between Sara and Lucio, the mother and son who are rediscovering one another. But at the end of the act word comes of Diego's resurrection – the injection that restored the rabbit to life has worked on a human being as well. With this news come the fearful implications of what this means, summed up by old Cico:

Do you understand – he was dead and he doesn't know anything. Where did he go? He ought to know that and he doesn't. And if he doesn't even know anything about his own death, that's a sign for anyone who dies that there isn't anything else. There's just nothing.

The final image of the act is that of Diego stumbling past, silent and terrified, watched in horror by the others.

Act III begins just a few moments later. Diego's family and friends gather together, talking about what has occurred, and in this frightened group, one person unexpectedly makes a declaration of faith. Lucio announces his intention to rejoin the priesthood, and explains why:

> He's there! He's there! Now I understand, and I really feel the meaning of Christ's word *Charity*. Because men cannot always stand upright, and so God wants his true House to be on earth, promising true life over there. In that Holy House where the tired and the poor and the weak can kneel, and where all pain and all pride can kneel too. Like this, Monsignor,
> (*kneeling*)
> before you, now that I feel myself worthy again to put on my vestments for the divine sacrifice of Christ and for the faith of men.

The others are perplexed by Lucio's sudden return of faith, but he refuses to explain further, merely stating simply that 'In God there is no death'. At this point there is the sound of a shot. Diego, announcing now that since there is no God there is no reason and he is free to do whatever he wants, has finally given vent to his fury and tried to kill Arcadipane. He is disarmed and comes face to face with

Lucio. The tables have been turned – the self-righteous father and unwilling son have changed, and in their places are a man racked with doubt and a priest burning with faith in his vocation. Lucio confronts Diego with the wrongs he has done, with his past failures and inadequacies, and Diego asks for help. The help Lucio offers is rebirth:

> You must come back from the dead, father. Don't you see? You closed your eyes to life because you thought you could see another life over there. This has been your punishment. God blinded you and now lets you open your eyes . . . .

Restored to life, able to see himself and the others around him, Diego is finally able to let Lia go to Sara, her mother. The play ends with Cico declaring that a miracle has taken place.

Unlike *The New Colony*, where the action is dominated by a single figure, La Spera, there is no one protagonist in *Lazarus*. Diego Spina is the focus of attention in that he dies physically and is resurrected, but the action of the play is dominated by Sara and Lucio. Lucio also undergoes a resurrection, when he comes to terms with the power of love in its irrationality and recovers his vocation. Thus there are three rebirths in the play: Diego's physical restoration, Lucio's realization of the meaning of faith, and Diego's coming to terms with his own past that finally allows him to break free of his own repressions. Sara, on the other hand, is the one character who is whole throughout the play. Talking to Lucio in Act II, she tells him of the joy she feels at meeting him again:

> I am truly liberated. I don't want for anything, because

I have it all. I don't hope for anything because what I do have is enough for me: I have my health, my heart is full of peace and my mind is calm.

Sara's contentment is in direct contrast to Diego's state of mind, both before and after his death, but there is a basic contradiction at the heart of the portrayal of Sara. For her happiness has been achieved by a rejection of bourgeois society *and* by transcending the harsh realities of peasant life. Silvana Monti explains it in the following terms:

> Sara's happiness cannot be reached within a bourgeois or peasant community, but only through a metahistoric relationship with the earth and with a man like Arcadipane, who has no real connotations and seems to have stepped straight out of popular folk tales. So once again Pirandello denies the possibility of any kind of social or political regeneration. Man is saved as being of unique value, but not man as a rationalising creature desperately searching for truth. The man saved is 'orgiastically' steeped in natural rhythms.[9]

Silvana Monti's point is important, because she shows that, as with *The New Colony*, Pirandello is declining to posit any valid alternative. *Lazarus* glorifies faith, the irrational and the supernatural; the final miracle of regeneration is as much a *deus ex machina* as the earthquake and flood which save La Spera. The miracle may renew the lives of the characters of the play, but it offers no wider message of hope. In the Bible, the miracle of Lazarus is an example of the power of faith, but in Pirandello's play, which appeared in the same year as *Tonight We Improvise*, the miracle is one more stage gesture. The happy ending does not come about through man's own efforts, but through belief in the irrational. The actress playing Mommina gets up after her stage death and walks away, emphasizing the transitoriness of illusion. In *Lazarus*, Pirandello seems to be offering that same illusion as a straw to clutch at, in view of the failure of any alternative form of social order.

'The Mountain Giants'

Pirandello began writing *The Mountain Giants* in 1929, but had still not finished the play by the time of his death in 1936. It was performed one year later in 1937 in the Boboli Gardens in Florence, but unquestionably the most famous production of this play was the version directed by Giorgio Strehler at the Teatro Lirico, Milan in 1967. Pirandello's son, Stefano, has put together details of the unwritten final act and, as Strehler points out in his programme note, the unwritten end 'offers the possibility of transforming a work', an extraordinary opportunity for any director.

The Mountain Giants is one of Pirandello's most important works and yet it is also one of the least known outside Italy. He described it in a letter to Marta Abba as his masterpiece, explaining also that

The mountain giants are the triumph of fantasy, the triumph of poetry, but at the same time also the tragedy of poetry in this brutal, modern world.

The play may be seen as a statement of Pirandello's disillusionment with the role of art in contemporary society, a position towards which he had been moving steadily for many years. Pirandello had deeply involved himself in exploring the apparent dichotomy between art and life, between form and motion, and had come increasingly to investigate this duality in theatre terms, and yet at the same time he had sought the illusory ideal solution offered by the ideology of Fascism. The incompatibility between these two viewpoints accounts for the increasing sense of tension and uneasiness in Pirandello's writing in the late 20s and early 30s, and nowhere is that tension expressed more powerfully and explicitly than in *The Mountain Giants*.

In this play all notion of a naturalistic setting has disappeared. The action takes place in a surreal world, in the fantastic villa Scalogna inhabited by a grotesque group of mad people, led by Cotrone a wizard and illusionist. Into this group come a company of travelling actors who, driven by Ilse, the leading lady, are trying to popularize the posthumous work of a young poet who killed himself for love of her. The title of this work is *The Changeling*, and when the actors begin to perform it in Section III (the missing section would have been Section IV), we realize that it is indeed Pirandello's own play of the same name. Cotrone proposes to the company that they should present their play for the wedding festivities of the mountain giants and, in the missing final section, they agree to this. A makeshift stage is rigged up with a curtain round a tree, in an open space in front of the Giants' houses, and the actors prepare for their play. But the Giants' servants, symbols of materialism and tastelessness, do not want Ilse's poetic play. They demand entertainment, a song and dance routine, with no pretensions to high art. Although Cromo, the character actor, tries to persuade the others to acquiesce to the audience's demands, Ilse refuses. She attacks the audience for their ignorance and in their rage and intolerance she is torn to pieces behind the tattered curtain of her stage.

In his programme notes to the play, Strehler suggests that Pirandello schematized various modes of acting in the figures of Cotrone, Ilse and Cromo.[10] Ilse, he argues, is 'the mission carried out, the martyrdom'. She represents an ideal of high art that sees itself as divorced from practical considerations, and is dedicated to the work in which she performs rather than to the needs of her audience. One is reminded of Eleonora Duse insisting on performing D'Annunzio's plays to dwindling audiences because she believed absolutely in their aesthetic value. Cromo, in contrast, represents 'theatre-trade'. He is a true professional, willing to supply whatever his audiences ask of him. Cotrone, who is not part of the company but one of the 'Scalognati', is the actor–director for whom life is theatre. The 'miracles' he creates are a means of coping with the wretchedness of existence. In Act II, he invites Ilse and her company to remain in the villa, and to try and look at the world with the eyes of belief in illusion:

> No need to reason any more! We live on that up here. We have nothing, but we have all the time in the world for ourselves; that's indescribable wealth, an absolute ferment of dreams. Things around us speak and have meaning only in the arbitrary way in which we choose to alter them in our desperation. Our kind of desperation, mark you.

In the villa the inhabitants create their own illusions. Later in the same scene, Cotrone explains to Ilse that whilst the actors play their parts and make phantasms come to life, the 'Scalognati' do the opposite and turn their own bodies into phantasms. As Strehler puts it: 'Cotrone sums up all the possibilities of the theatre.'

Strehler is suggesting that the play cannot be simply

interpreted in terms of binary oppositions, a common pattern in much of Pirandello's earlier work. The issues are not presented through dichotomy, as, for example in *Six Characters*, nor is Pirandello so concerned with notions of relativity. *The Mountain Giants* is a play about the function of art, about the role it is able to play in a world of sadness and misery. Cotrone, on the one hand, and the group in the villa, represent what Strehler calls 'pure theatre', the creative spirit that springs straight from the poet's mind. Ilse and the actors represent the theatre of actors: performance theatre. They take a text and interpret it, but they do not create that text prior to the performance. Strehler points out that this kind of distinction reflects the distinction between text and performance, the two components that together make up theatre.

Ilse and her company are taking a playtext around in search of an audience, but Cotrone has withdrawn from audiences, and thus withdrawn from any attempt to communicate with the world outside the villa. As he explains to the others in Section II, he has given up and removed himself from all the trappings of human society:

> Look at the earth, what a sad and sorry sight! Maybe there's someone down there who's under the delusion that he's living our life; but it isn't true, of course. Not one of us is in the body that another person sees us in; we're in the soul that speaks from God knows where. No-one can know that. Appearance after appearance with this ridiculous name of Cotrone . . . and him, with the name of Doccia . . . or Quaqueo . . . A body is death: shadow and stone. Woe to anyone who thinks he can see himself in his body and his name!

Cotrone refers, throughout the play, to the innocence of animals and children, directly linking loss of innocence to growth of reason. Elsewhere in his writing, as in *The Rules of the Game*, for example, Pirandello had examined the sterility produced by a life based on reason. Cotrone has tried to escape from that sterility, into a world of his own making, a world in which heavenly beings can descend to earth, puppets can move and speak, dead men can return to life again. When Ilse begins to recite her part in Section III, she is joined by two characters, images that Cotrone tells her have materialized directly out of the imagination of the writer whose words she speaks. Again and again Cotrone warns against the deadening effects of reason and logical explanation. Existence can only be made tolerable, he suggests, by putting aside rationality and accepting what occurs without question.

In a different way, Ilse and the actors are also in revolt against rationality, but their revolt is one which causes pain and ultimately, death. When the actors first appear and tell Cotrone and the Scalognati about their play, Cromo describes the dead poet's work as a 'cancer that has eaten us down to the bone'. Ilse's sense of mission has become a fanaticism as extreme as that of Sirio Dossi in *Diana and Tuda*. It has become an obsession so total that eventually she dies for it, without ever understanding the meaning of Cotrone's remark about the dead poet: 'Anyone who's a poet writes poems and doesn't kill himself.' Ilse is, in a way, Tuda, continuing the struggle after the death of the artist. 'I have given to his work the life that he was denied', she tells Cotrone. She sees herself as a life-bringer, the bearer of a special message that can transcend death; significantly the play she is trying to perform is a fairy story about a mother and child. In *The New Colony*, the mother figure was saved, but in this play not even she survives. There is no *deus ex machina* in *The Mountain Giants* to bring about a final climax, for this is probably Pirandello's most consciously dialectical play.

Strehler has pointed out the way in which this play discusses the relationship between text and performance, and between different attitudes to theatre. What the play also deals with is the vast complex area of communication in the theatre. Cromo, as the actor willing to play whatever he is asked, turns theatre into a commodity for the consumption of mass audiences. Ilse, in contrast, sees her own relationship with the text as pre-eminent and fails to understand the need to establish any basis for mass communication. Cotrone, as he admits, has opted out of the whole business of trying to communicate. In rejecting civilization as he knows it, he can afford to create a separate, introspective world for himself and the 'Scalognati', beyond institutionalization.

In opting out of the struggle, refusing to put himself in the position that eventually kills Ilse, Cotrone emerges as a more likeable kind of Hinkfuss character, one whose anti-rationality arouses our sympathy. Ilse, in comparison, is the suffering, fanatical figure whose obsession with her ideal of pure art finally destroys her. But Ilse is in search of an ideal, she suffers for it and finally dies for it; the nobility of her actions, which are motivated by love, stands in contrast to Cotrone's retreat from the world. Ilse's nobility contrasts also with the baseness of her destroyers – the servants of the Giants, sent down the mountain because their masters were too busy with 'important matters'.

In *The Mountain Giants* there is no straightforward right and wrong position. Cotrone's case is presented sympathetically and we are invited to consider the validity of his views by reflecting on the squalid inadequacies of the world as we know it. Ilse, the female protagonist, is almost driven mad by her obsession, but she represents the case for the continuation of the institution of art. Both she and Cotrone make theatre, but only Ilse and her actors see theatre as necessarily involving a text, performers, a playing space and a public. That they disagree on the priority of those elements is another issue, for the fact remains that they try to continue a tradition and have not chosen an easy road into a world determined by their own exigencies and desires.

Through this play Pirandello seems to be debating with himself, between the needs of the soul for space and boundless imagination, as expressed by Cotrone, and the responsibility of the artist to the life that inspires his work. Because it is his last play, and because it was unfinished when he died, subsequent readings of the play have been framed within that notion of incompleteness. It is easy to draw parallels with *The Tempest*, and to recall the popular belief that Prospero's final speech is a farewell to the theatre, for Cotrone is in many ways a Prospero figure, conjuring spirits from the air. But Prospero was continually plotting to rejoin the world and to take up his role in society, whereas Cotrone has put the world behind him.

Pirandello described *The Mountain Giants* as both the triumph and the tragedy of poetry. In an earlier letter to Marta Abba he stressed his belief in the play and his hope that its greatness would be recognized:

> With it I shall go down, all the way down into the very entrails of despair. If the public doesn't weep this time, it means their hearts are turned to stone.

The full force of that tragedy emerges if we consider *The Mountain Giants* as the culmination of Pirandello's work, as his final pronouncement on the role and function of art. For this is a play that offers no answers to the problems it raises, and the lack of answers reflects the impossibility of reconciling an ideal of art with a repressive ideological system. Pirandello tried hard to keep his art separate from his politics, but although he may have managed to avoid making overt political statements, he could not avoid the inevitable consequences of the dominance of a Fascist discourse. The intellectual game of playing life off against form in theatre terms gradually took on deeper implications in his work, as can be seen by the way in which the idea of struggle begins to be replaced by the idea of resignation to adverse circumstances. The characters in Pirandello's earlier plays argue, question, suffer and try to fight back, but the characters in the Myths are more fatalistic, resigned to the greater force of circumstance. Moreover, in the Myths there is always an ideal world of Nature that the individual, once removed from the corruption of modern society, might be able to inhabit – La Spera's island, Sara's farm, Cotrone's villa – a place of withdrawal from struggle.

It would be too simplistic to say that Pirandello's later plays represent a decline in his powers as a writer as his own personal disillusionment increased. What can be seen in the later plays is the tension resulting from the incompatibility of an art form that originates from questioning and an ideology based on an ideal of authoritarian order. On the one hand Pirandello was trying to create a universal theatre, whilst on the other hand he was making public statements in support of Mussolini's invasion of Abyssinia. In his final plays the absurd size of the gulf between those two elements in his

6
The Search for Theatre Forms

No study of Pirandello's explorations of theatre form would be complete without a consideration of his experiments with the one-act play. His very first attempt at writing for the theatre in 1898 was a one-act play, *L'epilogo* (*The Epilogue*) which was published in that year but not produced. In 1910 Nino Martoglio, the Sicilian playwright and producer, directed two short plays by Pirandello: *The Epilogue*, now entitled *La Morsa* (*The Vice*) and *Lumie di Sicilia* (*Sicilian Limes*), thus beginning Pirandello's involvement with the professional theatre. His interest in the form of the one-act play continued for the rest of his life, with *Sogno, ma forse no?* (*A Dream, But Perhaps It Isn't*) being written in 1931 and only performed in Italy in 1937 after his death. In his Foreword to his translations of Pirandello's one-act plays, William Murray declares that a close reading of these thirteen little dramas will provide an excellent survey in miniature of Pirandello's work as a playwright.[1]

With his continued interest in the one-act play, Pirandello clearly felt that it was a form that should not be underestimated. His experiments with the full length play were matched by his experiments with the shorter format, culminating in his dream play of 1931. The fact that so many of the one-act plays should be well known testifies to Pirandello's skilful handling of this type of theatre.

The one-act play must necessarily have a much tighter focus than the longer play. It is a form suited to the vignette, either comic or tragic, to the rapid build-up of climax and anti-climax. Because the dénouement comes so quickly, the attention of the audience must be closely held and the plot developed with brisk, strong strokes, for dispersal weakens the structure and risks turning it into a pallid imitation of the full length play. The one-act form is also an ideal vehicle for the interior monologue, where a single character dominates the action. In short, although the one-act play cannot have the range and scope of the full length work, it can create an intensity and focus that would be hard to achieve with greater length. A useful comparison might be made between the vast interplay of light and shadow in a Canaletto canvas, for example, and the precisely detailed focus of individual vignettes within the painting. Taken out of context, some of Canaletto's group scenes can exist wholly in their own right with no need of external referents. Once seen in their overall frame, the focus shifts and the relationship of the individual units with the whole totally changes their meaning.

'Sicilian Limes'

In his early one-act plays Pirandello shows discipline and control, stressing certain key elements of plot and characterization. The same interest in the distinction between private honesty and social exigencies that can be seen in his earlier full length drama can also be seen in his early one-act plays. The motif of adultery appears, as do the motifs of deceit for personal gain, disappointment, thwarted social aspirations and betrayed promises. Perhaps because of the intensity of focus on individuals there appears to be a greater sense of bitterness in the one-act plays. In *Sicilian Limes* for example, the play centres upon the frustrated hopes of Micuccio, a Sicilian peasant who has travelled up to the north of Italy to honour a promise to Sina, the girl he hoped to marry. Sina has become a successful singer, thanks largely to Micuccio's early help. When Micuccio arrives at Sina's house, she is too busy with her wealthy friends to see him, and keeps him waiting in an anteroom. When she appears, bejewelled and wearing a very low cut gown, Micuccio is shocked at the change in her, having imagined her to be the village girl he remembered from the past. Realizing that she has now moved into a world in which he has no part, Micuccio leaves, but not before he has forbidden Sina to touch the bag of limes he has brought as a gift, and has stuffed the money he brought to honour his debt down the neck of her dress in token of her fall from purity.

The action of the play follows the period from Micuccio's arrival to the moment of his departure and during that time we see the gradual growth of doubt in his mind and his increasing sense of abandonment. Micuccio is presented as a good man, upright and honest, in contrast to the selfishness of Sina who cannot even spare the time to leave her guests to come and speak to him after he has travelled for thirty-six hours to reach her. His plight is made even more pitiful by the device of freeing the audience from all illusions about Sina long before Micuccio's belief is destroyed. At the start of the play, Ferdinando and Dorina, the servants, make fun of him behind his back as he tells the story of his past attachment to the woman he calls Teresina but who, significantly, has chosen to shorten it to the more fashionable Sina.

The play tells the story of one man's disappointed hopes, but it also has more far-reaching implications. The action is built on the problem of shifting class status – Sina has changed her class position through her sudden rise to fame, whereas Micuccio has remained locked into the position in which he was born, but Pirandello seems to be suggesting that such rapid change produces undesirable results. Sina has sold herself and her principles to attain her present power. The purity of honest village life is symbolized by the bag of limes that Micuccio has carefully carried with him. When he forbids Sina to touch that gift, he does so because he feels that she has betrayed the values of village life, but also because through that betrayal she has changed her identity. She has ceased to be the woman he once knew, the woman of his imagination. When Sina appears for the first time, interrupting the conversation between Micuccio and the friendly old lady, Zia Marta, he is dumbfounded:

> What she's done to herself . . . it . . . it doesn't seem real to me . . . All . . . all . . . like that . . . (*Referring to Sina's nudity, but with disbelief, not scorn*). A dream . . . her voice . . . her eyes . . . It isn't . . . it isn't her anymore . . . .

Sicilian Limes is about the corruption of innocence, the betrayal of the simple, honest way of life by the wealth-hungry world of the cities. It is a motif central to Pirandello's thought – the characters in the villa Scalogna of *The Mountain Giants* are in flight from the evils of modern society, for example. But Pirandello was also fully cognizant of the evils of village life, and if he occasionally allowed himself the luxury of looking for an idealized pastoral setting, he could also be darkly realistic.

'The Other Son'

L'altro figlio (*The Other Son*) is a play about the more savage human emotions. First published as a short story in 1905, it belongs very much to the *verismo* school and recalls the work of Luigi Capuana. It was not produced as a play, however, until 1923, when Ferdinando Paolieri revized the text. It was performed in Tuscan.

The action of the play is set in a poor Sicilian village. An old, illiterate peasant woman, Maragrazia, lives in poverty, refusing all contact with her son, Rocco, who is relatively prosperous. Her other two sons have emigrated to America and she lives in hope of them helping her one day, writing pathetic letters to them through the medium of Ninfarosa, the village letter-writer. All her love and affection are given to the silent, absent sons, none to the one nearest at hand. This behaviour is so inexplicable to the village women that they treat her as someone slightly mad. The arrival of a young doctor, a middle class figure with an educated background, provokes a cataclysm. He discovers that the letter-writer has been deceiving the old woman, not bothering to write her letters at all, and expresses his disgust at such behaviour. Ninfarosa, defending herself, tells him how Maragrazia neglects her own son, and when he meets that son soon afterwards, the doctor's belief in Maragrazia's madness is strengthened. Rocco comes across as a caring man, hard-working, honest and plain-speaking, who shows more bitterness about the way his brothers ignore their mother than about the way his mother ignores him.

The mystery of Maragrazia's rejection of her son is therefore at the centre of the play, and is only revealed in the horrific finale. Driven finally to tell the doctor her own version, Maragrazia explains in a lengthy monologue how her son was conceived as the result of a brutal rape. She had gone to look for her missing husband, only to find him murdered by a gang of bandits whom she discovered playing bowls with the decapitated heads of their victims. Their leader had shown her her own husband's head, but had been murdered in his turn by Rocco's eventual father. Imprisoned for three months until he was finally brought to justice, bound, gagged and repeatedly raped, Maragrazia had conceived her unwanted child. The climax of her monologue, which is also the climax of the play, relates how the child was born:

I swear to you I would have torn out my insides so as not to give birth to that child. I knew I could never have stomached holding it. Just thinking about feeding it at my breast made me scream like a mad thing. I wanted to die. My mother, bless her soul, never even let me see it. She took it away to his relatives who brought it up. Now doctor, don't you think that I can truly say he's no son of mine?

When the doctor points out that Rocco is in no way to blame, Maragrazia agrees. She will say nothing against him, but cannot bear the idea of him because of what he recalls for her. He is the horror of her past experiences re-embodied, just as her absent sons are embodiments of the void at the centre of her life.

The Other Son recalls the dark world of Giovanni Verga's stories, the world where the individual is helpless in the face of the power of the brutal forces of nature and has to become hard in order to survive. The play shows many levels of cruelty, conscious and unconscious, with the device of the outsider, the doctor, used as a means of exposing the harsh facts of Maragrazia's story. Her monologue is the key point of the play, where she towers over what has gone before, dwarfing all other arguments by the power of her tale.

The format of the play is that of the detective story. We are presented with a mystery, with an educated young detective figure and finally with a shocking dénouement. Maragrazia's revelation solves the immediate question of why she rejects her son, but opens up whole new vistas. In one stroke, presumed madness is transformed into the tragedy of lives cruelly destroyed by an act of violence in which both mother and child are innocent victims. The rational world that man attempts to construct for protection provides no safety at all against the force of the irrational. It should not be forgotten that the essay 'On Humour' dates from 1908, only three years after the writing of the original story. In his essay Pirandello focuses on the abyss between the individual's need for reassuring structures and the inexorability of existence that can sweep away all illusions.

The Other Son ends on a note that relates directly to the essay 'On Humour'. Having told her story, Maragrazia returns to the world of the present, where she protects herself by believing in the love of her absent sons. As the play ends, she leaves the stage with the Doctor who has promised to write a letter for her, rebuilding her illusion once again. So the play ends not on a darkly tragic note, but on a more humorous one: Maragrazia's survival instincts lead her to pick up where she left off. She will go on writing, go on trusting in others to send her letters, go on believing that her sons have not forgotten her, for only within the structures of this illusion can she find any comfort.

'The Man With the Flower in His Mouth'

The need of the individual to create a shell of illusion within which to exist is given a new twist in one of Pirandello's most famous one-act plays, *L'Uomo dal fiore in bocca* (*The Man With the Flower in His Mouth*). First published as a short story under the title 'Caffe notturno' ('Night café') in 1918, it then appeared in the Mondadori edition as 'La morte addosso' ('Living with death'). It was first produced as a play with its title revized yet again, in Rome in 1923.

The action of the play takes place in a café, where the Man with the Flower strikes up a conversation with a man who has just missed his train. It is late at night and both seem to have time to kill, but while the one complains about his missed train, the other starts to talk about things in a manner that seems increasingly odd. He talks at length about minutiae – the wrapping of a parcel in a shop, the furnishing of doctors' waiting rooms, but gradually moves onto a darker note –

> Because, my dear fellow, we all feel this terrible thirst for life, even though we don't know what it consists of. It's there, like a constant sore throat that can never be soothed, because life, at the moment we experience it, is

always so full of itself that we can never actually taste it.
All we can really savour is the past, which remains alive
within us.

With this expression of inner pain, the Man with the
Flower becomes increasingly agitated, until his final
revelation that he is afflicted with a fatal cancerous
growth:

Come here . . . I'll show you something . . . Look here,
under my moustache . . . here, see that pretty violet
mole? Do you know what it's called? Oh a lovely name,
sweeter than caramel – *Epitelioma* it's called. Say it,
hear how sweet it sounds: *epitelioma* . . . It's death, you
see. Death passed my way, planted this flower in my
mouth and said: 'Look after it, friend, I'll be back in 8
to 10 months time.'

The play is essentially a monologue, broken by the
occasional interjected questions and observations of the
Traveller, and by the two fleeting appearances of the wife
of the Man with the Flower, spying on him from behind
the corner of the street. The action of the play is therefore
concentrated in the words uttered, and on the way in which
the Man with the Flower strips off his veneer of social
politeness to lay bare the naked terror of advancing death.
The juxtaposition of the horror of his story and the almost
casual way in which the conversation between the two men
begins gives the play its power. Unlike Maragrazia's tale,
which provided the answer to questions posed within the
play, the Man with the Flower's story *is* the play. All the
emphasis is on his psychology, on the way in which the fear
of death has driven him beyond human emotions. He
rejects his wife's love, could even, as he says 'just snuff out

171

the life in some total stranger . . . pull out a gun and kill someone like yourself who just happens to have missed his train'. He has become anarchic, capable of irrational action because life has ceased to be meaningful for him. This powerful image of the doomed man spending his remaining time in the shops and cafés of his petit bourgeois world is one of the most striking in all Pirandello's opus.

Plays and Prose Narrative

The Man With the Flower in His Mouth offers a good example of the processes whereby Pirandello transformed a prose text into theatre.[2] As a short story, the narrator/speaker is the Man with the Flower, and most of his speeches have been lifted verbatim from the prose text. What Pirandello has done in the play is to add precise directions for long pauses to break up the language, and has built up the character of the Traveller as a foil to the Man with the Flower. What had been a monologue as a short story is therefore transformed into an exchange between two characters, during which time the audience is able to relate both to the Man with the Flower's predicament *and* the Traveller's embarrassment. The device of the wife who twice peeps round a corner and is spotted by the Man with the Flower is a further attempt to move the play away from its form as a prose monologue.

In his essay 'Spoken Action', written in 1899, Pirandello stresses the close relationship between prose and theatre, pointing out the heavy reliance of contemporary theatre on prose narrative sources. He also emphasizes the difficulties of transforming a prose text into theatre, arguing that 'every descriptive or narrative prop has to be abolished on a stage'. For what he calls the 'miracle' of the

transformation to occur, a new language must be
developed:

> a language that is itself spoken action, a living language
> that moves, the expression of immediacy, at one with
> action, the single phrase that must belong uniquely to a
> given character in a given situation: words, expressions,
> phrases that are not invented but are born when the
> author is fully at one with his creation so as to feel what
> it feels and want what it wants.

Sandro d'Amico[3] in an article tracing Pirandello's
gradual involvement in theatre, suggests that the theatre
was a logical conclusion for him to reach. The idea of a
form in which an actor attempts to represent another
human being, to 'fix' a character within the boundaries of
the play, becomes a paradigm for Pirandello's view of the
human condition. The actor pretends to be someone else –
man, Pirandello suggests, is forced into a series of
disguises in order to avoid the naked terror of a desolate
existence. Moreover, the transitory nature of the theatre,
where characters come briefly alive for the duration of the
play reflects Pirandello's theory of the inexorability of the
destructive flow of time.

But as Pirandello seems to be hinting in 'Spoken
Action', he was not only drawn to the theatre for reasons
of its symbolic value in his own intellectual system. He
gradually came to write more for the theatre with a view to
altering the focus of his material. The loss of what he calls
narrative props in theatre leads to very different emphases.
In his 1918 essay on 'Theatre and Literature', he points out
that the work of art in its written form and the play
performed by actors are necessarily different. If the actor
is to become more than a mouthpiece for the author, he

must create new life in his role. The task of the author is therefore to provide material to which the actor will give form and expression. So the relationship between written play text and performance may be compared to the relationship between prose narrative and play, where the bones of the story may provide the material for the author to create something completely new.

Narrative Stage Directions

Many critics have noted that in spite of his insistence on the differences between prose and play writing, Pirandello reveals his predilection for narrative in his stage directions. Like Bernard Shaw's, Pirandello's stage directions go far beyond indications for actors and directors, and give details of the psychology of characters, and information about the action, or express value judgements. Above all, Pirandello's stage directions expose a precisely articulated point of view, as in this example from *Henry IV*:

> *A long pause. In the throne room it begins to get dark, increasing the sense of uneasiness and deepening consternation of the four men in disguise, distancing them still further from the principle Player, who stays apart from them, contemplating a terrifying mystery that involves not only him but all humanity.*

The information contained in this passage goes beyond what is necessary for the staging of the scene and assumes a narrative function, a frequent feature of all Pirandello's plays. At times the stage directions have nothing but a narrative function, as in this extract from *Tonight We Improvise*:

The curtain goes up again.
Dr. Hinkfuss begins to beat about the bush.
*'It might be a good idea,' he must have thought, 'to
start out by giving a synthetic representation of Sicily
with a little religious procession. It'll add a bit of
colour.'*

Here the directions provide insight for the reader into the
motivation of Hinkfuss; it is important to remember that
the precision of Pirandello's writing enabled him to
produce texts that could both be read and be used by actors
for performance. Theatre, for Pirandello, was also
literature, and good writing, he suggests, must exist *both*
as stage material and as a literary text, thus implying a
reader. 'The work of art is what remains,' he says in his
Address to the Volta Congress on Dramatic Theatre in
1934, 'even though it lives for an instant in the transitory
performance given in a theatre.'

Experimental One-Act Plays

In many of the one-act plays which derive from earlier
stories, the use of stage directions is part of the conscious
process of adapting the prose source into a new form. In a
few cases, however, Pirandello has used the one-act format
to try and break new ground, most notably in his dream-
plays, *All'uscita* (*At the Exit*) and *Sogno, ma forse no?* (*A
Dream, But Perhaps It Isn't?*).

At the Exit was first published in 1916, but only
produced in 1922. It is not so much a dream-play as a ghost
play, set in a country cemetery, peopled by the dead who
have 'left their useless bodies in their graves'. The ghost of
the Fat Man meets that of the Philosopher, a Laudisi-type
figure who discourses on the futility of life and dominates

the first half of the play. Then the Fat Man tells the Philosopher about his past life, when he was betrayed by his wife and came, in death, to understand the feelings of his rival. He predicts that his wife will be murdered by her lover, and almost immediately she rushes in, covered with blood, and tells the story of her own violent end. The three figures are then joined by the apparition of a child eating a pomegranate which he refuses to share. As he finishes it, he disappears and the Philosopher explains:

> The pomegranate was his last desire. He clung to it with both hands. He was all there, in those last few morsels he hadn't yet tasted.

The Murdered Woman begins to weep, and immediately the Fat Man vanishes too, his last desire fulfilled. The Murdered Woman and the Philosopher are left behind, the one desperate and distraught, the other calm and rational. At this point a live peasant family cross the stage, providing a sharp contrast with the hopelessness of the apparitions. The play ends with the Murdered Woman running after the peasant family, vainly trying to embrace a living child, as the Philosopher leans against a tree remarking that he is afraid he will always remain where he is, still reasoning.

The Murdered Woman and the Philosopher, who might almost be blueprints for Silia and Leone Gala in *The Rules of the Game*, symbolize the conflicting forces of passion and reason. She is doomed never to realize her one desire – to love and be loved completely, while he cannot cease to reason. The Child and the Fat Man realize their desires and free themselves from them, but the desires of both the Murdered Woman and the Philosopher are impossibly far-reaching and they are doomed even after death.

Pirandello classified this grim little play as a 'profane mystery'. It belongs to that line of the European tradition of the dream-play or ghost play that is located in a world immediately after death, a kind of limbo. Interestingly, the stage directions emphasize the appearance and behaviour of the characters and do not call for lighting effects or other devices to reinforce the image of other-worldliness. The peasants are described as 'solid', but no indications are provided on how that solidity should be created in stage terms.

In contrast, *A Dream, But Perhaps It Isn't* is full of elaborate stage directions, prompting at least one critic to attack Pirandello's 'tendency to overstress theatricality'.[4] The play was first produced in Lisbon in 1930, and performed in Italian in 1937 in Genoa. It is related to the ballet scenario, *The Salamander*, which Pirandello wrote in 1928 for the Turin Company of the 'Teatro della Pantomima Futurista'.

In *A Dream*, Pirandello uses layering techniques in a manner similar to that of Borges. The central figure, the Young Lady, who is the dreamer, is involved in two relationships, and part of the dream expresses her feelings of guilt and of fear at her lover's jealousy. In the opening moments of the play, the lover materializes as a figure in a nightmare:

> . . . *a hand, an enormous hand, emerges from under the couch now converted into a bed and raises up the lowered part of it. And as the back of the couch gradually rises into place, a man's head, also enormous, emerges behind it. The expression on the huge head is one of terrible distress: the hair is tousled, the forehead wrinkled into a deep frown, the eyes terrifyingly gloomy and fixed in a hard menacing stare. It is a face out of a horrible nightmare.*

Later in the play she dreams that her lover is strangling her. The stage is plunged into darkness, and when the lights go up again, the Young Lady is seen in the process of waking, rubbing her neck with the recollection of the dream. She is awakened by a knocking on the door, which turns out to be a waiter who brings her a gift from her second lover, a pearl necklace. Almost immediately, the first lover arrives, and tells her that he had hoped to buy her the necklace, but it had been sold when he went to the shop. The play ends with the couple drinking tea together, the man unsuspecting of the Young Lady's betrayal, the Young Lady trying to seem casual and unconcerned.

The play raises a number of questions that remain unanswered. The horror of the Young Lady's dream, which occupies two-thirds of the action and culminates in her death, could be seen as premonitory. As the play ends on a note of false optimism, with the game of deceit just beginning, the audience is left with doubts about the eventual outcome. The dream sequence has provided a possible logical ending to the relationship we see emerging between the two characters. On the other hand, the emotive power of the dream sequence so colours our perceptions of the final scene that we are unable to divorce reality from that dream. As the title suggests, the line between what is and what is imagined is too fine to be drawn with any accuracy.

A Dream is full of stage effects, lighting changes, masks, transformations both of scenery and of gesture (the Man is dreamed into motionlessness or robotic movements at various points in the play). Plot, as such, is secondary to theatrical devices, and the engendering of terror in the first part of the play becomes the dominant activity. One feels that Pirandello went as far as he could with the one-act format in this play, stretching its limits towards the visual and pantomimic, and away from the narrative. Whereas many of his plays not only derive from prose sources but could also be paraphrased in prose, *A Dream* belongs very definitively to theatre and relies on additional sign systems to extend the purely verbal.

If an introductory study of a writer as prolific as Luigi Pirandello is to attempt more than plot summaries of his works, a process of selection must be employed and some plays must, regrettably, go undiscussed. Pirandello's work is multi-faceted, still fraught with problems for theatre critics and biographers alike. The task of re-evaluating his writings has only just begun. It would be encouraging to hope that the revival of interest in his plays in Italy by critics and theatre practitioners alike would lead to similar revivals elsewhere so that Pirandello might be *seen* to be one of the great seminal dramatists of the twentieth century in practice as well as in reputation.

References

1. Introduction

1. Clive Barker, 'Right You Are, (If You Could Only Think So)' in *The Yearbook of the British Pirandello Society*, no. 1 (1981) 26–35.

2. Eric Bentley, *Naked Masks*, (New York: Dutton, 1952) p. 349.

3. Jennifer Stone, 'Mirror Image/Collage: Reality, Representation and Revolution in Pirandello', in F. Barker *et al.* (eds), *1936: The Sociology of Literature* (University of Essex, 1980).

4. Gaspare Giudice, *Pirandello, A Biography* (London: OUP, 1975). The English translation is an abridged version.

5. Olga Ragusa, *Luigi Pirandello, An approach to his theatre* (Edinburgh: Edinburgh University Press, 1980).

6. I am grateful to both Sandro d'Amico and Jennifer Lorch for discussing this matter with me. Jennifer Lorch's findings on the Pitoëff production formed the substance of her address to the British Pirandello Society in May, 1981 at the University of Bristol.

7. Dario Niccodemi, quoted in Diego Fabbri, 'Pirandello poeta drammatico' in *Atti del Congresso internazionale di studi pirandelliani* (Conference in Venice, 1961; pub. Florence: Le Monnier, 1967).

8. A. Tilgher, 'Life Versus Form' in J. Cambon (ed.), *Pirandello, A Collection of Critical Essays* (Englewood Cliffs, New Jersey: Prentice-Hall, 1967) pp. 19–34. From *Studi sul teatro contemporaneo* (Rome: Libreria di Scienze e lettere, 1923, 1928).

9. Martin Esslin, 'Pirandello: Master of the Naked Masks,' in

References

Reflections. Essays on Modern Theatre (New York: Doubleday & Co., 1971) pp. 47–57.

2. The Theatre-in-the-Theatre Plays

1. Landor McClintock, *The Age of Pirandello* (Bloomington: Indiana University Press, 1951).
2. Erving Goffman, *Frame Analysis: An Essay on the Organisation of Experience* (London: Penguin Books, 1974).
3. Luigi Squarzina and Gino Rizzo, 'Directing Pirandello Today', interview in *Tulane Drama Review*, x, 3 (Spring 1966) 76–90.
4. Edoardo Bruno, *Dialettica del teatro* (Roma: Bulzoni, 1973) pp. 93–105.
5. Raymond Williams, *Modern Tragedy* (London: Chatto & Windus, 1966) p. 156.
6. Patrice Pavis, *Problèmes de sémiologie théâtrale* (Montreal: Les Presses de l'Université du Québec, 1976).

3. Playing with Truth/Life?

1. Diego Fabbri, 'Pirandello poeta drammatico' in *Atti del congresso internazionale di studi pirandelliani 1961*, 37–49.

4. The Mask of Identity

1. Roger W. Oliver, *Dreams of Passion, the Theatre of Luigi Pirandello* (New York: New York University Press, 1979) p. 12.
2. Vaclav Hudecek, *ITI World Theatre*, xvi, 4 (1967).
3. Walter Starkie, *Luigi Pirandello, 1867–1936* (Berkeley and Los Angeles: University of California Press, 1967; 1st pub. 1926) p. 184.
4. Michel Foucault, *Madness and Civilisation* (London: Tavistock, 1964) p. 95.
5. Leonardo Bragaglia, *Interpreti pirandelliani* (Roma: Trevi Editore, 1969).
6. Jennifer Stone, 'Beyond Desire: A Critique of Susan Sonntag's Production of Pirandello's *Come tu mi vuoi*' in *The Yearbook of the British Pirandello Society*, I (1981) 35–48.
7. Quoted in the Introduction to *The Mountain Giants and other Plays by Luigi Pirandello*, translated by Marta Abba (New York: Crown Publishers Inc., 1958) p. 25.

References

5. Myth and Fable

1. Nino Borsellino, 'Il mito dell'arte, o il messaggio dell'impossibile', in Enzo Lauretta, ed., *I Miti di Pirandello* (Palermo: editore Palumbo, 1975) pp. 29–45.

2. Nicolas Evreinoff, *The Theatre in Life* (London: Harrap, 1927) This volume was prepared by Evreinoff for English-speaking readers out of his previous writings spanning some fifteen years work.

3. Starkie, *Luigi Pirandello*, op. cit.

4. Interview in *Il Tevere*, 16 March 1928, quoted in Giudice, p. 181.

5. Sandro d'Amico, 'Appunti per una diversa lettura critica e teatrale dei miti', in E. Lauretta, (ed.), pp. 100–104.

6. Giovanni Sinicropi, 'The Later Phase, Towards Myth', *Italica* XXXVIII (4 Dec. 1961) 265–95.

7. Renato Simoni, *Corriere della sera*, 19.4.1928, quoted in Bragaglia, p. 343.

8. See S. Bassnett-McGuire, 'Pirandello's British Première', in *Yearbook of British Pirandello Society*, II (1982).

9. Silvana Monti, 'Il teatro del Novecento nei tre "Miti" pirandelliani', in E. Lauretta, (ed.) (1975) pp. 67–89.

10. Giorgio Strehler 'The Giants of the Mountain', *World Theatre*, XVI, no. 3 (Special Pirandello number, May–June 1967) 263–9.

6. The Search for Theatre Forms

1. W. Murray, *Pirandello's One-Act Plays* (New York: Samuel French, 1970).

2. Of Pirandello's 43 plays, 29 derive from earlier prose writings. Of these prose writings 26 are short stories, while the remaining 3 derive from episodes in novels (*Liolà* having as its source an episode in *He was Mattia Pascal*; *Six Characters* deriving from a story and from a draft of a novel entitled *The Six Characters* and written in 1910; and *The New Colony* based on an episode from the novel *Suo Marito* (*Her Husband*) (1911).

3. Sandro d'Amico, 'Itinerario di Pirandello al teatro' in *Il Veltro*, XII, 1–2 (1968) 81–97.

4. Achille Mango, 'Funzione della didascalia nell'atto unico' in Stefano Milioto, ed., *Gli atti unici di Pirandello* (Agrigento: Edizioni del Centro Nazionale di Studi Pirandelliani, 1978).

Bibliography

The standard edition of Pirandello's works is *Opere di Luigi Pirandello* Milan, Mondadori. Volumes cited in this book are *Maschere nude*, 2 vols (1958); *Saggi, poesie, scritti varii* (1960; 2nd enl. edn 1965; 3rd enl. edn 1973).

Play translations

Three Plays of Pirandello (London: Dent; New York: Dutton, 1922). Contains *Six Characters in Search of an Author*, tr. E. Storer, *Right You Are (If You Think So)* tr. A. Livingston, *Henry IV*, tr. E. Storer.

Each in His Own Way and two other plays (London: Dent; New York: Dutton, 1923). Contains *Each in His Own Way*, *The Pleasure of Honesty*, *Naked*, tr. A. Livingston.

The One-Act Plays of Luigi Pirandello (New York: Dutton, 1928). Tr. E. Abbott, A. Livingston and B. V. Mitchell.

A Dream, But Perhaps Not (*This Quarter*, II, 4, June 1930) tr. S. Putnam.

As You Desire Me (New York: Dutton, 1931) tr. S. Putnam.

Tonight We Improvise (New York: Dutton, 1932) tr. S. Putnam.

Diana and Tuda (London: Samuel French, 1950) tr. Marta Abba.

Naked Masks, ed. E. Bentley (New York: Dutton, 1952). Contains *Six Characters in Search of an Author*, tr. E. Storer, *Henry IV*, tr. E. Storer, *It is So (If You Think So)*, tr. A. Livingston, *Liolà*, tr. E. Bentley and G. Guerrieri, *Each in His Own Way*, tr. A. Livingston.

Bibliography

Six Characters in Search of an Author (London: Heinemann, 1954) tr. F. May.

The Mountain Giants and other plays (New York: Crown, 1958) tr. Marta Abba. Contains *The Mountain Giants*, *The New Colony*, *When Someone is Somebody*.

Tonight We Improvise (London: Samuel French, 1960) tr. C. Fredericks.

Pirandello's One-Act Plays (Garden City, New York: Doubleday, Anchor, 1964) tr. W. Murray.

Pirandello, Three Plays (Penguin Books, 1969). Contains *The Rules of the Game*, tr. R. Rietty, *Henry IV*, tr. F. May, *Right You Are (If You Think So)*, tr. F. May.

Henry IV (London: Methuen, 1978) tr. J. Mitchell.

Six Characters in Search of an Author (London: Methuen, 1979) tr. J. Lindstrum.

General

Useful bibliographies may be found in:

A. Barbina, *Bibliografia della critica pirandelliana 1889–1961* (Florence: Le Monnier, 1967).

E. Bentley, *Naked Masks* (New York: Dutton, 1952).

T. Bishop, *Pirandello and the French Theatre* (New York University Press, 1960).

Pirandello's *Short Stories* ed. and tr. F. May (London and New York: OUP, 1965).

W. Starkie, *Luigi Pirandello* (London and Toronto: Dent, 1926; 3rd edn, Berkeley: University of California Press, 1965).

Worth consulting, but clumsily organized are:

A. Illiano, *Introduzione alla critica pirandelliana* (Verona: Fiorini, 1976).

O. Ragusa, *Pirandello: an approach to his theatre* (Edinburgh University Press, 1980).

Periodicals

Modern Drama, VI 4 (1964).

Forum Italicum I 4 (1967).

Italica XLIV 1 (1967).

World Theatre, XVI 3 (1967).

The Yearbook of the British Pirandello Society, no. 1 (1981), no. 2 (1982).

Bibliography

Criticism and Biography

A. C. Alberti, *Il teatro nel fascismo* (Rome: Bulzoni, 1974). Contains illuminating documents on Pirandello's relationship with Fascism.

S. Bassnett-McGuire, 'Art and Life in L. Pirandello's *Questa sera si recita a soggetto*', ed. J. Redmond, *Drama and Mimesis* (Cambridge University Press, 1980).

L. Bragaglia, *Interpreti pirandelliani* (Rome: Trevi, 1969). Gives details of Italian performances of Pirandello's plays.

O. Büdel, *Pirandello* (London: Bowes and Bowes, 1966). 'Studies in Modern European Literature and Thought'.

A. L. de Castris, *Storia di Pirandello* (Bari: Laterza, 1962).

G. Cambon (ed.), *Pirandello* (Englewood Cliffs, N.J.: Prentice-Hall, 1967). Useful collection of critical essays, including important pieces by R. Brustein and F. Fergusson, with extracts from A. Tilgher's seminal work on Pirandello.

M. Esslin, *Reflections* (Garden City, New York: Doubleday, 1969).

G. Giudice, *Luigi Pirandello* (Turin: U.T.E.T., 1963). Tr. as *Pirandello: A Biography* (London: OUP, 1975). (*Note*: The English version is not as extensive as the Italian.)

F. L. Lucas, *The Drama of Chekhov, Synge, Yeats and Pirandello* (London: Cassell, 1965).

L. McClintock, *The Age of Pirandello* (Bloomington: Indiana University Press, 1951).

J. Moestrup, *The Structural Pattern of Pirandello's Work* (Odense: Odense University Press, 1972).

A. Paolucci, *Pirandello's Theater: The Recovery of the Modern Stage for Dramatic Art* (Southern Illinois University Press, 1974).

J. Stone, 'Mirror Image/Collage: Reality, Representation and Revolution in Pirandello', in F. Barker et al. (ed.) *1936, The Sociology of Literature* (University of Essex, 1980).

R. Williams, *Modern Tragedy* (London: Chatto & Windus, 1966).

D. Vittorini, *The Drama of Luigi Pirandello* (Philadelphia: University of Pennsylvania Press, 1935).

Index

187

Index